THE ULTIMATE
WORLD
WAR II
QUIZ BOOK

THE ULTIMATE
WORLD
WAR II
QUIZ BOOK

1,000 QUESTIONS AND ANSWERS
TO TEST YOUR KNOWLEDGE

KIERAN WHITWORTH

Michael O'Mara Books

First published in Great Britain in 2017 by
Michael O'Mara Books Limited
9 Lion Yard
Tremadoc Road
London SW4 7NQ

A CIP catalogue record for this book is available from the British Library.

Papers used by Michael O'Mara Books Limited are natural, recyclable products
made from wood grown in sustainable forests. The manufacturing processes
conform to the environmental regulations of the country of origin.

ISBN: 978-1-78243-822-9 in paperback print format
ISBN: 978-1-78243-823-6 in ebook format

1 2 3 4 5 6 7 8 9 10

Front cover, clockwise from top left: EA 36319, CH 19, TR 1643, A 14612, E 18474,
E 18980, LN 6194, TR 2828, AP 56388, FRE 1001TR 453, E 21337
Back cover, clockwise from top left: TR 185, B 10172, BU 6674, TR 2043, CH 1401,
MH 13118, TR 2835, BU 11149
All images © IWM.

Designed and typeset by DESIGN 23
Maps by David Woodroffe

Printed and bound by CPI Group (UK) Ltd, Croydon, CR0 4YY

iwm.org.uk
www.mombooks.com

Contents

Introduction

World War II was a truly global conflict. Decades later its impact can still be seen in popular culture through the many books, movies and television series that provide a glimpse into the events that were witnessed by those who lived through it.

The experiences of most people in the war were unique. A soldier fighting in the desert had a very different experience to that of a sailor on a long voyage through an Arctic winter, or of a marine fighting on a lush tropical island. As fewer people who remember these historical events first-hand remain, it is important to continue to explore the facts about the war, and to try to understand the lessons of this key period of modern history.

This *Ultimate World War II Quiz Book* covers the global nature of the war, beginning with the events which led to war, going on to explore the conflict on each continent across land, sea and air, and also asking questions about the aftermath of the war in 1945. There are 1,000 questions to test everyone's knowledge, from someone who may remember a few facts from their schooldays, to those who feel more at home with the details. Some questions look at strategy, whilst others look at key technology, personalities or daring operations. The questions come in different forms: some simply require an answer, some are multiple choice, and others – in true military scrambled code – offer the answer in an anagram. These are placed in italics after the question. There are also questions based on photos, all from the Imperial War Museums' collection, and occasionally, you are even given a clue! In asking and answering the many questions contained within this book, the experiences of those who witnessed this truly global conflict will continue to be remembered by all of us today.

Imperial War Museums (IWM) is a family of five museums in the United Kingdom that cover modern conflicts since 1914. IWM's story of World War II does not just come from its vast archives of photographs, artwork, film, documents, objects and personal stories, but from the museums themselves. Historic sites such as Churchill's War Rooms, HMS *Belfast* and IWM Duxford provide visitors with the chance to walk in the footsteps of those who lived during the war, and to see how these important sites played a vital role in this global conflict.

CHAPTER 1

Before the War Began

1. What was the name of the treaty signed at the end of World War I which re-drew national borders in Europe?
   A) Treaty of Fontainebleau   B) Treaty of Versailles
   C) Treaty of Vincennes.

2. Where and when was the treaty signed that shaped post-World War I Europe and what international body did it create?

3. Which fascist leader came to power in Italy in 1922? *Boils nio minutes.*

4. What was the nickname for the fascist activists in Italy as seen in this photo?

5. In what year did Adolf Hitler come to power in Germany?
   A) 1929 B) 1931 C) 1933.

6. Truth or fiction? Hitler's popularity was in decline when he came to power in Germany.

7. Hitler replaced which leader in 1934 to become Führer?

8. What does the term 'Nazi' mean?
   A) National Socialist German Workers' Party
   B) National Unionists German Workers' Party
   C) Nationalists of Germany Socialist Workers' Party.

9. Which financial institution crashed on 29 October 1929, leading to the collapse of the international economy?

10. What was the name of the large shanty towns which formed in the United States during the global depression in the 1930s, and after which person were they named?

11. In what year did Germany withdraw from the League of Nations?   A) 1931   B) 1932   C) 1933.

12. Who was elected US president in 1932?
    A) Franklin D. Roosevelt   B) Herbert Hoover   C) Harry Truman.

13. In what year did Prohibition end in the United States?
    A) 1923   B) 1933   C) 1943.

14. In 1935, Hitler announced German re-armament and the re-introduction of what?

15. Truth or fiction? In order to train pilots, Germany used gliders rather than planes, so as not to break re-armament conditions.

16. On 3 October 1935, Italy invaded which country?
    A) Libya   B) Algeria   C) Ethiopia (Abyssinia).

17. Which disputed territory, a demilitarized zone, are these German troops marching into in 1936?

18. Truth or fiction? Adolf Hitler had an English aunt whom he visited in Britain after World War I.

19. Who is pictured here in 1938?

20. Following his meeting with Hitler in 1938, at which airport did the plane carrying the British prime minister arrive in Britain? A) Heathrow B) Heston C) Biggin Hill.

21. What phrase did the British prime minister say after returning from talks with Adolf Hitler in 1938?
A) 'No deal without peace' B) 'Peace in our time'
C) 'Peace not war'.

22. Which event led to the arrest of Adolf Hitler for treason in 1924? *Chit chums pun.*

23. In which prison did Adolf Hitler work on his political memoir?

24. What was the name of the political memoir that Adolf Hitler wrote whilst in prison?

25. In his political memoir, Adolf Hitler described the need for *Lebensraum*, but what was it?

26. What year did the Spanish Civil War begin?

27. What was the original name of Joseph Stalin, who would lead the USSR during World War II? *Dogs if jashz hiluvi.*

28. Joseph Stalin came from a family that ran what type of business?   A) Butchers   B) Cobblers   C) Blacksmiths.

29. In which country in the Russian Empire was Joseph Stalin born?

30. What did Joseph Stalin launch in the USSR in 1928?
A) The Two-Year Plan   B) The Five-Year Plan
C) The Ten-Year Plan.

31. Truth or fiction? The people who fell out of favour with Joseph Stalin were erased from history. For example, Nikolai Yezhov, head of the secret police, was erased from official photographs.

32. Who defeated Hitler in the German presidential elections in 1932?

33. Who said in 1931, 'Whoever can conquer the street will one day conquer the state'?

34. What was the name of the German-speaking area of Czechoslovakia which Hitler demanded in 1938?

35. What was the name given to Britain's policy of accepting German expansion in Europe in the 1930s?
A) Agreement   B) Aggrandizement   C) Appeasement.

36. Which German city was the site of talks between Britain, Germany, France and Italy during the Czechoslovakia crisis? Clue: this city was where Hitler attempted to seize power in 1923.

37. Which city in central Europe, situated on the Vltava river, are these German troops entering in April 1939?

38. In March 1939, following the occupation of Czechoslovakia, Britain and France guaranteed which country's independence?

39. To serve as a port for Polish trade, what was the former German city of Danzig (present-day Gdansk) established as? A) Trading city B) Open city C) Free city.

40. Which German foreign minister met with the Polish ambassador to discuss Danzig's return to Germany in October 1938? *Tom in chain vero probbj.*

41. Brown-shirted Nazi paramilitaries were known by which two-letter initials? A) SS B) SD C) SA.

42. Who was the leader of the Nazi 'Brownshirts'?

43. What name was given to the removal and murder of Nazi Stormtroopers on 29 June 1934? A) Night of the Long Grass B) Night of the Blades C) Night of the Long Knives.

44. In February 1933, which prominent building in Berlin broke out in flames?

45. What is being signed in this photograph?

46. With which country did Britain enter into a formal military alliance on 25 August 1939?
A) France B) USSR C) Poland.

47. In what year did Berlin host the Olympic Games?

48. Truth or fiction? A secret protocol in the Nazi–Soviet pact left Hitler free to attack Poland without risking war with the Soviet Union.

49. Which country was the only one to boycott the Berlin Olympics? A) Britain B) USSR C) Greece.

50. Truth or fiction? No Jewish athletes won medals at the Berlin Olympics despite many competing.

51. How many gold medals did African–American athlete Jesse Owens win at the Berlin Olympics?
A) Three B) Four C) Five.

52. Truth or fiction? During the Berlin Olympics, anti-Jewish signs were temporarily removed and anti-Semitic newspapers were taken off public display in Berlin.

53. What does 'radar' stand for?
A) Radio and data results B) Radio detection and ranging
C) Radio direction and range.

54. What was the name given to the chain of early warning stations built in the 1930s along the south and east coasts of England to detect enemy aircraft?

55. Name the air defence system set up by Britain prior to World War II? *To wed his gem dynst.*

56. American journalist William Shirer wrote in his diary: 'I'm afraid the Nazis have succeeded with their propaganda.' What was he referring to? (©The Estate of William Shirer)

57. In September 1931, Japan invaded and occupied which area of China?

58. What name did Japan give to the province of China they occupied in 1931?
A) Manchu B) Manchukuo C) Manchufu.

59. In January 1932, Japanese forces attacked by land, sea and air which Chinese city? *Nags hiah.*

60. What was the Chinese name of the Chinese Nationalist Party and who was the leader from 1925?

61. The Sino–Japanese war began in which year?
A) 1935   B) 1936   C) 1937.

62. Which two groups suspended their civil war to fight the Japanese invasion of China?

63. What was the name given to the atrocities perpetrated by Japanese troops in December 1937, when they captured the Kuomintang capital?

64. In Britain, how many gas masks were issued before war broke out?   A) 24 million   B) 34 million   C) 44 million.

65. Truth or fiction? In 1935, Australian prime minister Billy Hughes predicted the war in his book *Australia and the War Today*.

66. Which Italian king named Mussolini prime minister after the fascist leader threatened to march on Rome with his fascist followers in 1922?

67. Truth or fiction? In Italy in 1925, Mussolini proclaimed himself *Il Supremo*.

68. In 1932, Italy used which two African countries to provide a base for the invasion of Ethiopia?

69. Name the emperor of Ethiopia crowned in 1930. *Less see hail ai.*

70. In 1936, Italy relied on superior weapons against poorly armed tribes in Ethiopia, but which weapon did the Italians use that turned public opinion against Mussolini?

71. Name the German city where the Nazi Party rally in this photograph took place in 1938.

72. What name and abbreviation was used for the black-shirted security forces, a personal guard for Hitler, who replaced brown-shirted Stormtroopers in Germany?

73. Which memorandum was believed to have been produced at a conference in 1937 that was attended by Hitler and his closest advisors?
A) The Munich Memorandum
B) The Hossbach Memorandum
C) The Berlin Memorandum.

74. Which town (B), located in Northern Spain, was bombed by German and Italian aircraft on 26 April 1937 during the Spanish Civil War?

75. Which artist produced a famous painting of the Spanish town that was heavily bombed on 26 April 1937?

76. Name the right-wing Nationalist movement set up in Spain in 1933 and based on the Italian Fascist movement. *Lean gaf.*

77. Name the general who led a coup in Spain in 1936 following the election of a left-wing government.

78. What was the name of the Spanish Nationalist Army flown in to Spain by German and Italian aircraft?
A) Army of Spain   B) Army of the People   C) Army of Africa.

79. During the Spanish Civil War, Nationalists were supported from the air. What was the name of the German air contingent? Clue: it was named after a large bird.

80. Truth or fiction? In Spain, fighting broke out in Barcelona between rival factions in the Republican movement.

81. What name was given to foreign volunteers, pictured here, who fought for the Republicans in the Spanish Civil War?

82. What did Britain introduce in May 1939 due to growing German territorial expansion?

83. What name is given to the period 1936 to 1938 in the USSR, which saw the state target political opponents and the army?
A) The Great Purge   B) The Great Peace   C) The Great Terror.

84. A 1932 Nazi party election poster promised people in Germany *Arbeit, Freiheit und Brot*. What did this slogan mean?   A) Peace, freedom and bread
B) Work, freedom and bread   C) Work, faith and bread.

85. Which leader said in April 1923, 'The truth is that men are tired of liberty'?

86. In Europe in the 1930s, where did the term 'fascist' come from?

87. Name the British politician who formed the British Union of Fascists in the 1930s. *So mawls do ley.*

88. During the Spanish Civil War, how many foreign volunteers joined the fighting with the International Brigades?
A) 5,900   B) 59,000   C) 590,000.

89. What phrase was used by Hitler to explain the reasons for Germany's loss in World War I?

90. Name the woman who was Hitler's companion from 1932 and whom he would eventually marry in 1945. *Va ba rune.*

91. This Berlin synagogue is one of many Jewish properties that were attacked during which Nazi pogrom on 9–10 November 1938?

92. Why was the pogrom on 9–10 November 1938 given its name?

93. Between 1938 and 1939, nearly 10,000 children fled the persecution of Jews and other groups in Germany, and were brought to Britain. What were these evacuations called?
A) *Kindertransport* B) *Reichtransport* C) *Freiheittransport*.

94. Which German filmmaker famously captured the 1934 Nazi congress at Nuremberg, in the film *Triumph of the Will*? *Hasten rifle nile.*

95. Name this Berlin landmark, which was damaged by fire in 1933.

96. German infantry are pictured crossing the Austro–German border in 1938. What name is commonly used for the German annexation of Austria in 1938?

97. What was the name of the song that became the official anthem of the Nazi Party?

98. Truth or fiction? Hitler strengthened his power by having Germany's army swear an oath of allegiance to him.

99. The Nuremberg Laws were passed in Germany in 1935. What three things did they do?

100. In September 1934, Adolf Hitler proclaimed what in Germany? A) Conscription B) The Nazi salute to be used by the army C) Start of the Thousand-Year Reich.

101. Which German politician was chief of Nazi Party propaganda? *Sop gob jels beeh.*

102. What did insignia with a double lightning flash, used to denote the SS, imitate?
A) Electricity B) Runic characters C) Saluting.

ANSWERS

1. B) Treaty of Versailles.

2. The Hall of Mirrors at Versailles on 28 June 1919. The treaty led to the creation of the League of Nations.

3. Benito Mussolini.

4. Blackshirts.

5. C) 1933.

6. Truth. His electoral support was in decline when he was invited to form a coalition government.

7. President Paul von Hindenburg.

8. A) National Socialist German Workers' Party.

9. Wall Street.

10. Hoovervilles, named after President Herbert Hoover.

11. C) 1933.

12. A) Franklin D. Roosevelt.

13. B) 1933.

14. Conscription. This was prohibited under the Treaty of Versailles.

15. Truth. Many pilots in the fledgling air force were trained on gliders.

16. C) Ethiopia (Abyssinia).

17. The Rhineland, the demilitarized buffer zone between Germany and France.

18. Fiction. Whilst it is true that Hitler had a British sister-in-law, her claims that he visited relatives in Liverpool have been widely dismissed as fanciful.

19. British Prime Minister Neville Chamberlain, returning after his meeting with Hitler in Munich in September 1938.

20. B) Heston.

21. B) 'Peace in our time.'

22. Munich Putsch.

23. Landsberg prison.

24. *Mein Kampf.*

25. Living space for the German people to be created by establishing an empire in the east.

26. 1936.

27. Josif Dzhugashvili.

28. B) Cobblers.

29. Georgia.

30. B) The Five-Year Plan, a campaign to boost Soviet industry.

31. Truth. He was erased from official photographs when he fell out with Stalin in 1939.

32. Paul von Hindenburg.

33. Joseph Goebbels.

34. Sudetenland.

35. C) Appeasement.

36. Munich.

37. Prague, on 20 April 1939.

38. Poland. Britain and France believed it would be Hitler's next territorial ambition and began military planning.

39. C) Free city. Danzig was run by the League of Nations and lack of access to the port created resentment in Germany.

40. Joachim von Ribbentrop.

41. C) SA, standing for *Sturmabteilung* or 'Stormtroopers'.

42. Ernst Röhm.

43. C) Night of the Long Knives.

44. The Reichstag. Hitler used the fire at the German parliament to make the Nazi Party the only legal political party in Germany.

45. The Russo–German Non-Aggression Pact.

46. C) Poland.

47. 1936.

48. Truth. It was intended to divide Eastern Europe into German and Soviet spheres of influence.

49. B) USSR.

50. Fiction. Several Jewish athletes won medals.

51. B) He won four medals: for long jump, 100 metres, 200 metres and 4×100-metre relay.

52. Truth. Anti-Semitic newspaper *Der Stürmer* was one such paper taken off public display.

53. B) Radio detection and ranging.

54. Chain Home (CH) stations.

55. The Dowding System, named after Fighter Command's commander-in-chief, Air Chief Marshal Sir Hugh Dowding.

56. 1936 Berlin Olympics.

57. Manchuria.

58. B) Manchukuo.

59. Shanghai, responding to alleged Chinese attacks on Japanese areas of the city.

60. The Kuomintang or Guomindang, led by Chiang Kai-shek.

61. C) 1937.

62. The Chinese Nationalists and Chinese Communists.

63. The 'Rape of Nanjing'. The violence against the population of the city continued for six weeks.

64. C) 44 million. Gas masks were first issued in 1938.

65. Truth. He also pointed out that Australia was unprepared for war.

66. King Victor Emmanuel III.

67. Fiction. He proclaimed himself *Il Duce* or 'the leader'.

68. Eritrea and Somaliland.

69. Haile Selassie (he only adopted the name when he became emperor).

70. Poison gas.

71. Nuremberg.

72. The *Schutzstaffel* (SS), meaning 'defence echelon'.

73. B) The Hossbach Memorandum. It was used in post-war trials as evidence to show Hitler's plans for war.

74. Guernica. The town had been crowded for a market on the day of the bombing and there were no defences or shelters.

75. Pablo Picasso.

76. Falange.

77. General Francisco Franco.

78. C) Army of Africa.

79. The Condor Legion.

80. Truth. Moderates clashed with radical anarchists.

81. The International Brigades.

82. Conscription.

83. C) The Great Terror.

84. B) Work, freedom and bread.

85. Benito Mussolini.

86. The term 'fascist' derives from the Roman symbol *fasces*, which was a bundle of sticks (seen as weak on their own yet strong collectively), surrounding an axe (a symbol of authority). Italian blackshirts adopted this symbol in the 1920s.

87. Oswald Mosley.

88. B) 59,000.

89. 'Stab in the back'. Hitler believed the collapse was caused by socialist and Jewish factions which were part of an international conspiracy.

90. Eva Braun.

91. *Kristallnacht* or 'Night of the Broken Glass'.

92. It was named because of the shattered glass from thousands of Jewish businesses that were attacked by Nazis in towns across Germany.

93. A) *Kindertransport* or 'children's transport'.

94. Leni Riefenstahl.

95. This is the burnt-out dome of the Reichstag after the fire.

96. *Anschluss*.

97. *'Horst-Wessel-Lied'*, named after Horst Wessel, a Nazi Party activist who was shot in 1930 by two members of the Communist Party of Germany.

98. Truth. The army swore an oath of unconditional loyalty.

99. They stripped German Jews of their citizenship, forbade marriage between German and Jewish citizens, and removed Jews from the armed forces and civil service.

100. C) Start of the Thousand-Year Reich.

101. Joseph Goebbels.

102. B) Runic characters.

CHAPTER 2

Outbreak

1. In August 1939, Soviet forces defeated the Japanese in which battle?

2. Which German battleship was launched on Valentine's Day 1939? *Back mirs.*

3. What name was given to the alliance between Germany and Italy signed on 22 May 1939? Clue: this is a type of metal alloy.

4. What was the swastika symbol before being used by the Nazi Party?   A) Nordic runes   B) A symbol from Mayan civilization   C) A symbol from South Asia.

5. In June 1939, the SS *St Louis* was turned away from the United States. What was it carrying?
    A) Weapons   B) Typhoid   C) Jewish refugees.

6. King Zog was the king of which European country that was overrun by Italian forces in April 1939?
    A) Albania   B) Greece   C) Macedonia.

7. Who became Soviet foreign minister in May 1939? *Camels to havoy vlov.*

8. On 31 August 1939, German SS troops staged a fake attack, supposedly by Polish saboteurs, on a German radio station on the Polish border. Where was the station?
    A) Warsaw   B) Gleiwitz   C) Poznan.

9. Which German coast-defence ship is seen here firing on the Polish military depot at Westerplatte in September 1939? Clue: it's a German state.

10. Which British politician said in a radio broadcast in October 1939, 'I cannot forecast to you the action of Russia. It is a riddle wrapped in a mystery inside an enigma'?

11. Truth or fiction? After the Italian foreign minister, Count Ciano, was informed of German plans to attack Poland in August 1939, he urged Mussolini not to join Germany in the approaching war and to remain neutral.

12. Britain's ultimatum to Germany to end hostilities in Poland expired at 11 a.m. on 3 September 1939. When did France's ultimatum expire – before or after Britain's?

13. What name was given to the German plan for the invasion of Poland?

14. During the invasion of Poland, Germany had how many army divisions guarding the border with France?
A) 44 B) 88 C) 144.

15. Which town (B) in Poland became the meeting place for Soviet and German forces during the invasion of Poland?

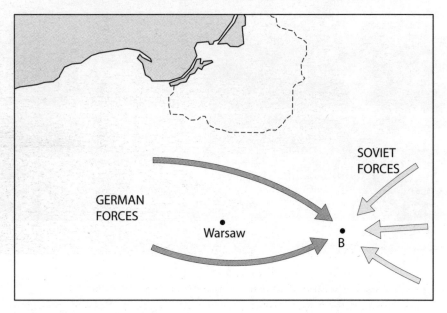

16. *Blitzkrieg* was the offensive method of war waged by Germany from the start of World War II. What did it mean?

17. The German Army was divided into two groups, North and South, for the invasion of Poland. Who commanded each army?

18. Following the invasion of Soviet troops into Poland on 17 September 1939, the Polish government and high command sought refuge in which neutral country?
A) Switzerland B) Romania C) Slovakia.

19. Soviet and German commanders discuss details of a demarcation line between the two armies in Poland. Which German general is in the foreground indicating the line on a map with his hand?

20. What was the name of the 1940 massacre by the Soviet secret police of Polish army officers following the invasion of Poland?

21. The Polish resistance which developed after the partition of Poland by Germany and Russia was known as what?
A) The Warsaw Uprising
B) The Home Army
C) The Army of Resistance.

22. What is the name given to this German dive bomber plane, used in close ground support as 'flying artillery'?

23. When Poland was invaded by Germany, was it vulnerable only on the Polish–German border, or was it exposed on other borders?

24. What is the name for the period of inaction in Europe after the defeat of Poland, lasting until April 1940? *Hey whope tarn.*

25. What name was given to the Russian–Finnish conflict which began on 30 November 1939?
A) The White War   B) The Snow War   C) The Winter War.

26. What was the formidable fortified barrier that Finland constructed on its southern border with the USSR?
A) Manfred Line   B) Mainio Line   C) Mannerheim Line.

27. What was mounted to German dive bombers and caused great psychological terror?
A) Powerful light mounted in the nose
B) Wind-driven siren   C) Mounted rockets.

28. What type of troops (pictured above) did Finland deploy against Soviet forces in the Russo–Finnish War?

29. Which Soviet general was replaced during the Russo–Finnish War in 1940, and by whom?

30. Truth or fiction? Britain and France wanted to help Finland and agreed to send troops to fight the Russians in 1939–40.

31. What was the name of the treaty which ended the Russo–Finnish War of 1939–40? Clue: it is a Russian city.

32. Truth or fiction? Warsaw radio continued to play the Polish national anthem continuously until the siege of Warsaw ended in September 1939.

33. General Tadeusz Kutrzeba, of the Warsaw garrison, is seen here negotiating surrender terms for the city. With which German general (middle background with moustache) is he negotiating?

34. Where did the negotiations for the surrender of Warsaw take place? Clue: it was in the Warsaw factory of a European car brand.

35. In 1939 the population of Canada was no more than 12 million. What percentage of its population would eventually join its armed forces during the war?
A) 1 per cent   B) 5 per cent   C) 10 per cent.

36. On 5 September 1939, what did President Roosevelt confirm in the United States?

37. During the first three months of the war in Britain, what led to the most number of deaths?
A) Air raids   B) The Blackout   C) Food shortages.

38. Name the German pocket battleship, seen here in flames, which was scuttled off Montevideo in Uruguay on 17 December 1939.

39. Which battle was fought off the coast of Uruguay between British naval forces and a German pocket battleship? *Table for the ravel tipet.*

40. Name the German captain who scuttled his battleship off Montevideo in December 1939, and what happened to him?

41. How old was Winston Churchill in 1939?   A) 64   B) 69   C) 71.

42. Truth or fiction? German U-boats were named after the German word for submarine, *Unterseeboot*.

43. Who was the naval commander of the German U-boat force?

44. Which British warship was sunk in Scapa Flow in October 1939? *Koar yoal.*

45. Which German region was briefly attacked by French forces in September 1939?
A) Rhineland B) Saarland C) Corland.

46. Truth or fiction? British air minister Sir Kingsley Wood refused permission to bomb German factories at the start of the war because they were private property.

47. Which three British ships engaged a German pocket battleship in the south Atlantic in December 1939?

48. British King George VI is seen leaving a bunker in this French fortification built in the 1930s to defend its border with Germany. What was the fortified line called?

49. In November 1939, what was 'sealed off' in Warsaw from the rest of the city?

50. In Britain, what was introduced on 8 January 1940? *Goat in rin.*

51. The plan by Britain and France to send troops to Norway in 1940 was initially to provide armed support for Finland, but what was another objective of the plan?

52. Which port in Norway became a target for Anglo–French forces in April 1940? *In krav.*

53. Which country was invaded simultaneously with Norway by German forces in April 1940?
A) Iceland   B) Sweden   C) Denmark.

54. Which German heavy cruiser was sunk by guns at the harbour fort in Oslo during the initial invasion of Norway?

55. Truth or fiction? Anglo–French operations in Norway were poorly equipped. Some French ski troops became unable to operate due to a lack of straps for their skis.

56. German forces seized what tactical advantage during the Norway invasion, which would ultimately allow them to defeat the Anglo–French forces there?

57. The King of Norway escaped to Britain in May 1940 to set up a government-in-exile. Who was he?
A) King Harald VII   B) King Harstad VII   C) King Haakon VII.

58. Following the Allied campaign in Norway, Neville Chamberlain resigned. Along with Winston Churchill, who was also a possible successor to Chamberlain? Clue: this is a town in northern England.

59. Winston Churchill became British Prime Minister on 10 May 1940. What other major event happened on this day?

60. What was Operation Alphabet?
A) An invasion of Iceland
B) German troops land in Greece
C) The evacuation of Allied troops from Narvik in Norway in 1940.

61. What types of troops were used by Germany for the first time in the war during the invasion of Nordic countries?

62. What codename was given to Germany's invasion of Norway in April 1940?   A) Operation *Weserübung*.
B) Operation *Weishaupt*   C) Operation *Weseling*.

63. What name was given to a 1905 German plan, which was adapted in 1940, for a German invasion of Belgium and The Netherlands (C), in tandem with a second invasion of France by German Forces further south (D), intending to trap Allied Forces in Northern France?

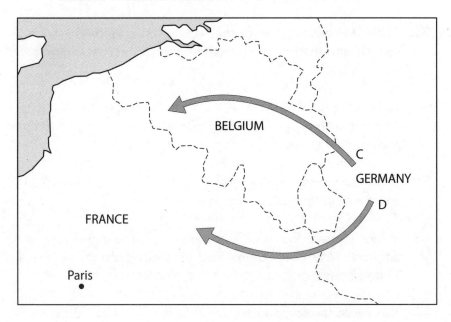

64. Where was the lightly defended, hilly and wooded area in Belgium through which German forces attacked in 1940?
Sad ner en.

65. Which Belgian fortification on the Albert Canal was captured by German troops on 10 May 1940?

66. Truth or fiction? During the invasion of France and the Low Countries, Germany had more tanks than the French.

67. Name the first major tank battle of World War II, fought on 12–13 May 1940 between German and French units?
A) Battle of Sedan   B) Battle of the Somme
C) Battle of the Gembloux Gap.

68. What was the name of the river where Anglo–French forces advanced to support the Dutch and Belgians in May 1940?
A) River Meuse   B) River Dyle   C) River Dender.

69. By dusk on 13 May 1940, German forces had established bridgeheads across the River Meuse at Dinant, Monthermé and which other location in France?

70. What name was given to the German plan for the invasion of France and the Low Countries?

71. Who replaced General Gamelin as leader of French forces during the Battle of France?   A) General de Gaulle
B) General Weygand   C) General Pétain.

72. Truth or fiction? German Army Group A, which was advancing through Belgium, was caught up in 270 km (170 miles) of traffic delays.

73. Which German panzer major-general led the main point of attack in May 1940 against France, and what book did he write about the use of tanks in modern warfare?

74. What was the name of Hitler's private train, which arrived close to the Belgium border on the morning of 10 May 1940? Clue: it's a country!

75. On 20 May 1940, German forces reached which French town, effectively dividing the Allied armies in two?
A) Abbeville   B) Amiens   C) Arras.

76. Name the commander of the British Expeditionary Force in France? *Dog tol rr.*

77. Operation Dynamo was the codename for what?

78. Which Dutch city was bombed on 14 May 1940, which led to mass casualties and the Dutch surrendering the next day?
A) Amsterdam   B) Rotterdam   C) Eindhoven.

79. Which British vice-admiral had been retired before the war but was recalled in 1939 and planned the evacuation of Dunkirk? *Say ben marrt rad.*

80. Why was Operation Dynamo given its name?

81. What was Operation Sickle Cut?

82. At which French town did British forces attempt to counterattack against German troops heading to the Channel coast?   A) Arras   B) Baupame   C) Cambrai.

83. Truth or fiction? In 1940, the port of Dunkirk in France was the largest port on the English Channel.

84. During the evacuation at Dunkirk, Captain William Tennant spotted which landmark with which to speed up the evacuation?   A) A lighthouse   B) A buoy   C) A mole.

85. In this photo, three of the 'little ships' can be seen. What was the role of the 'little ships' during the Dunkirk evacuation?

86. Truth or fiction? The only day during the Dunkirk evacuation when more men were rescued from the beaches than from the harbour was 30 May 1940.

87. Approximately how many men were rescued from Dunkirk by the end of the operation on 4 June 1940?
A) 138,000 B) 238,000 C) 338,000.

88. Who is believed to have predicted in June 1940, 'In three weeks England will have her neck wrung like a chicken.'

89. Which French hero offered the Germans an Armistice on 22 June 1940, forming a puppet government in France?

90. Where did the signing of the French surrender in 1940 take place? *Nope mé cig.*

91. Which junior French officer arrived in London on 18 June 1940, and would go on to lead Free French forces?

92. Which French spa town became the home of the French government following the defeat of France?
A) Livremont   B) Cluny   C) Vichy.

93. Which three values replaced 'Liberty, equality, fraternity' as the national slogan of the French government in 1940?

94. What country declared war on France on 10 June 1940?
A) Italy   B) USSR   C) Romania.

95. Following the defeat of France, what symbol was adopted by Free French forces?

96. Under the terms of the French surrender, which areas of France came under German occupation?

97. Which British merchant ship, shown in the photograph below, was used to evacuate troops from Saint-Nazaire in Brittany, but was sunk during the evacuation?

98. On 18 June 1940, Charles de Gaulle broadcast from the BBC in London. The date was also the 125th anniversary of which major battle?

99. One of the Dunkirk evacuation 'little ships' was owned by Commander C. H. Lightoller. What historical event was he also known for?   A) He was the King's second cousin B) He commanded at the Battle of Jutland C) He was the senior surviving officer of the *Titanic*?

100. Which Polish general led the Polish government-in-exile before dying in a plane crash in 1943?

101. Truth or fiction? Hitler personally gave the command to halt panzers on the western side of Dunkirk during the Battle of France.

102. General Heinz Guderian is standing in this photo taken during the Battle of France. What encryption machine can also be seen?

ANSWERS

1. The Battle of Khalkhin Gol.

2. *Bismarck*.

3. Pact of Steel.

4. C) A symbol from South Asia, where it had often been regarded as a good luck charm.

5. C) Jewish refugees. The 937 Jewish refugees aboard were forced to sail back to Europe.

6. A) Albania.

7. Vyacheslav Molotov.

8. B) Gleiwitz. Some concentration camp prisoners were killed by the SS and dressed in Polish uniforms. Their bodies were shown to the press, and the German response was the invasion of Poland.

9. SMS *Schleswig-Holstein*. It is believed to have fired some of the first shots of World War II.

10. Winston Churchill.

11. Truth. When war was declared, Italy announced its status as non-belligerent, as Mussolini despised the term 'neutral'.

12. After, at 5 p.m. on 3 September 1939.

13. *Fall Weiss* or 'Case White'.

14. A) Just 44 divisions. Hitler gambled that France would not mount an offensive to help Poland.

15. Brest-Litovsk.

16. 'Lightning War'. Tanks, artillery and motorized infantry, supported from the air, punched a hole through an enemy's defence on a narrow front, which was quickly exploited by rapidly moving forces.

17. General Fedor von Bock (Army North) and General Gerd von Rundstedt (Army South).

18. B) Romania.

19. General Heinz Guderian.

20. The Katyn Massacre. German forces found the mass graves of around 22,000 Poles in the Katyn Forest in 1943. Russia denied responsibility until 1990.

21. B) The Home Army.

22. The Stuka Ju (Junkers) 87.

23. Yes, the Germans were able to invade across Poland's borders with Bohemia, Moravia and Slovakia.

24. The Phoney War.

25. C) The Winter War.

26. The Mannerheim Line.

27. B) A wind-driven siren. This gave a loud wailing sound as the plane dived.

28. Ski troops. Finnish troops were clad in white winter camouflage and could move quickly in winter forest terrain.

29. Marshal Voroshilov was replaced by Marshal Timoshenko.

30. Truth. There was an agreement to send an expeditionary force to the Baltic.

31. The Treaty of Moscow.

32. Truth. The anthem was played for nearly three weeks before it stopped on 27 September 1939.

33. General Johannes Blaskowitz on 28 September 1939.

34. In the Skoda motor factory in the Warsaw district of Rakowiec.

35. C) 10 per cent.

36. The neutrality of the United States.

37. B) The Blackout. The rise in traffic accidents in the dark saw a major increase in deaths.

38. *Admiral Graf Spee*.

39. Battle of the River Plate.

40. Captain Hans Langsdorff. He shot himself in Uruguay once he had scuttled his ship.

41. A) 64.

42. Truth. *Unterseeboot* is German for 'submarine'.

43. Admiral Karl Doenitz.

44. *Royal Oak.*

45. B) Saarland. It was the only independent French offensive action of the war.

46. Truth. Despite some politicians calling for more action, British aircraft were initially ordered not to bomb targets in Germany.

47. *Exeter, Ajax* and *Achilles*. Despite being out-gunned, they succeeded in damaging *Admiral Graf Spee*, forcing the German ship to make to Montevideo.

48. The Maginot Line, named after French war minister André Maginot.

49. The Warsaw Ghetto. In October 1939, German occupying authorities established a Jewish ghetto.

50. Rationing. Rationing had been used in Britain during World War I, and some items such as petrol were rationed from the start of World War II, but it began in earnest in 1940 for food and clothing.

51. To cut off the flow of iron ore from neutral Sweden to Germany.

52. Narvik.

53. C) Denmark. Danish airfields were used to support the invasion of Norway.

54. *Blücher.*

55. Truth. They lacked straps.

56. German forces captured airfields.

57. C) King Haakon VII.

58. Lord Halifax.

59. The invasion of Belgium and the Netherlands by Germany.

60. C) This was the evacuation of Allied troops from Narvik in Norway in 1940.

61. Paratroopers.

62. A) Operation *Weserübung*.

63. The Schlieffen Plan, after its creator Graf Alfred von Schlieffen, chief of the Imperial German General Staff.

64. Ardennes.

65. Fort Eben-Emael. Defended by 1,200 men, the fort was captured by 78 airborne troops who landed by glider.

66. Fiction. France had more tanks but these were tied to slow-moving infantry divisions.

67. C) Battle of the Gembloux Gap.

68. B) River Dyle.

69. Sedan.

70. *Fall Gelb*, or 'Case Yellow'.

71. B) General Weygand.

72. Truth. Army Group A would go on to be a key component of the German attack and subsequent victory despite the traffic delays.

73. Major-General Heinz Guderian and the book was *Achtung-Panzer!*.

74. 'Amerika'.

75. A) Abbeville.

76. Lord Gort.

77. The plan by the Royal Navy for the evacuation of British, French and Belgian troops from the beaches of Dunkirk.

78. B) Rotterdam.

79. Bertrand Ramsay.

80. Vice-Admiral Ramsay worked in a room deep in the Dover cliffs that had once contained a dynamo, a type of electrical generator, and this led to the name.

81. The German plan to cut the Allied armies in two following the break-out from the River Meuse. It was to be a spectacular success for the Germans.

82. A) Arras. The counterattack failed.

83. Truth. It had about 8 km (5 miles) of quays. Due to air attacks the port was made largely unusable, forcing the Allies to also use 16 km (10 miles) of beaches to the north of Dunkirk to evacuate.

84. C) The East Mole. This allowed destroyers to come alongside and load greater numbers of troops.

85. To bring the men from the shore, primarily from the beaches, to the safety of larger vessels anchored offshore.

86. Truth. 29,512 men were collected from the beaches and 24,311 men from the harbour.

87. C) 338,000.

88. General Weygand.

89. Marshal Philippe Pétain.

90. Compiégne.

91. Charles de Gaulle.

92. C) Vichy.

93. 'Work, family, country'.

94. A) Italy.

95. The Cross of Lorraine.

96. Paris, the whole of northern France and the French Atlantic coast.

97. SS *Lancastria*. It is estimated that some 3,500 people died as a result of its sinking.

98. The Battle of Waterloo.

99. C) He was the senior surviving officer of the *Titanic*.

100. General Sikorski.

101. Fiction. General von Kluge gave the order on the evening of 23 May 1940. Hitler approved it the following day.

102. Enigma machine (left foreground).

CHAPTER 3

Standing Alone

1. Following the defeat of France, Hitler visited Paris on 28 June 1940. He was accompanied by a sculptor and two architects. Who were these men?

2. In June 1940, Hitler was concerned about the Soviet Union's seizure of the territories of Bessarabia and northern Bukovina. Where were these areas?
    A) Hungary   B) Romania   C) Serbia.

3. What was the British naval operation Catapult, which took place in July 1940?

4. Radar was a term coined in the United States in 1940, but what was the term for the British predecessor to radar?

5. Who was the commander of British naval forces that left Gibraltar to confront French warships in 1940? *Miser jill as memo vers.*

6. After defeating France, Hitler returned to Berlin to celebrate the victory. What term was coined for these state occasions?
    A) Führer luck   B) Führer weather   C) Führer time.

7. Which prototype British aircraft first flew in March 1936 from Eastleigh airport?

8. Name the British chief designer at Supermarine Aviation Works, responsible for designing the most famous British fighter of World War II? *Mirth jellc.*

9. Truth or fiction? The Spitfire was hand-built and took three times as long to build as the German Messerschmitt 109.

10. The Spitfire MK1A was the first all-metal, stressed-skinned fighter to go into production in Britain, powered by Rolls-Royce Merlin engines. What other key design feature did the plane become famous for?

11. Five Spitfire Mark I's of 19 Squadron are pictured here flying in starboard echelon formation. At which airfield were they based, which is now a branch of Imperial War Museums?

12. What nickname was given to the German Messerschmitt 109E by its pilots?   A) Devil   B) Gerbil   C) Emil.

13. What was the name of the German air force?
A) Luftflotten   B) Luftwaffe   C) Lufttag.

14. Truth or fiction? During the Battle of Britain, the Messerschmitt 109 fighter was only able to maintain 75 minutes' flying time over England.

15. Name the German World War I fighter ace who was head of Germany's air force. *In gög manrr hen.*

16. This photo shows the interior of the Sector 'G' Operations Room at Duxford. What crucial advantage did this air defence network provide that helped the RAF overcome the numerical superiority of the Germans in 1940?

17. Truth or fiction? In July 1940, just as the Battle of Britain was beginning, Britain was producing double the amount of fighters than Germany.

18. In early July 1940, the Germans began air attacks on shipping in the English Channel, Thames Estuary and North Sea. What name did the Germans give to this tactic?

19. On 12 August 1940, a German air raid damaged which radar station, the loss of which was concealed by radar stations elsewhere in Britain?
A) Heanor   B) Eastleigh   C) Ventnor.

20. Which RAF station (B), in 11 Group Fighter Command, was heavily bombed in August 1940 during the Battle of Britain?

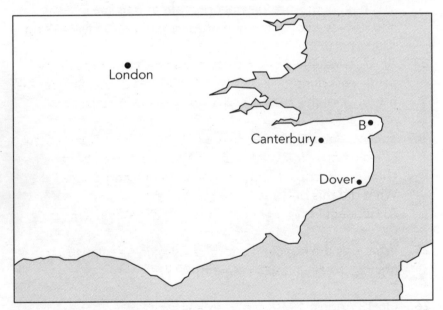

21. Name this British fighter aircraft, which shot down the most enemy aircraft during the Battle of Britain.

22. What was the nickname of the Dornier Do 17, which was the most numerous German bomber during the Battle of Britain? A) Flying Pencil B) Flying Coffin C) Flying Wing.

23. Air Vice-Marshal Keith Park commanded 11 Group in the south-east during the Battle of Britain. What country was he from? Clue: this is the 'land of the long white cloud'.

24. At the beginning of the Battle of Britain, British planes flew in V-shaped formations of three known as 'vics', but this was changed to copy the German system of flying in two pairs. What did this become known as?
A) Connect Four B) Finger Four C) Flight Four.

25. What was the codename for the German air offensive against Britain in the summer of 1940?

26. On 13 August 1940, the Germans attacked with the intention of knocking the RAF out of the war. What was this day called? A) Zero Day B) Eagle Day C) D-Day.

27. What nickname was given by German aircrews to the day 15 August 1940, when all three German air flotillas attacked across the length of Britain, suffering heavy losses? *Lhats rub cakdy.*

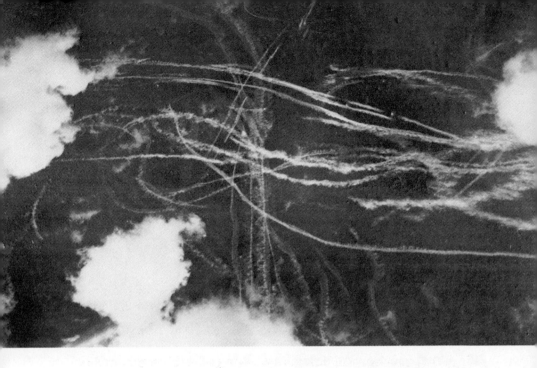

28. This photograph shows condensation trails or contrails that are left by aircraft in the sky during 'dogfights'. Which British war artist painted 'Battle of Britain', showing similar contrails in his painting?

29. Truth or fiction? During the Battle of Britain, one Polish pilot who bailed out of his aircraft landed at a lawn tennis club, where he was signed in, given a racket, and invited to take part in a match.

30. In this photo, pilots are running to their aircraft. What name was given to this type of rapid dispersal?

31. Who was the British Air Chief Marshal of Fighter Command during the Battle of Britain? *Hun words higgid.*

32. What were German plans for the invasion of Britain, proposed for September 1940, called?

33. Where was British Fighter Command's headquarters during the Battle of Britain?
A) Burnham Priory   B) Bentley Priory   C) Debden Priory.

34. During the Battle of Britain, members of the WAAF were vital and helped plot aircraft in operation rooms. What did WAAF stand for?

35. What happened to Josef František, a Czech pilot, during the Battle of Britain?   A) He was the first pilot to be killed
B) He was the only Czech pilot to shoot down a German plane
C) He was the highest scoring Allied pilot?

36. Which squadron number was given to the RAF Polish squadron during the Battle of Britain?
A) 103 (Polish) Fighter Squadron
B) 203 (Polish) Fighter Squadron
C) 303 (Polish) Fighter Squadron.

37. Name the air vice-marshal from South Africa who commanded 10 Group during the Battle of Britain. *Darnns quirin bit*

38. Truth or fiction? British radar stations could detect aircraft up to 80 km (50 miles) from the British coast.

39. Which British volunteers played a vital role in the defence of Britain by supplying aircraft positions? Clue: their name is a watching brief.

40. In May 1940, a radio broadcast called on British men to join a new force, the Local Defence Volunteer (LDV). By what other name was it known?

41. Which army numbered only 200,000 in 1939, but ended the war as the biggest ever volunteer army, with 2,500,000 men?
A) The British Indian Army   B) Army of Greece
C) The Turkish Army.

42. RAF pilots came from many countries to fight in the Battle of Britain. Which two neutral countries were also represented by pilots during the battle?

43. On 18 August 1940, RAF Fighter Command suffered an all-out attack which saw some of the largest losses on both sides during the Battle of Britain. What would this day later become known as?
A) The Shortest Day
B) The Deadliest Day
C) The Hardest Day.

44. Hermann Göring (centre) can be seen talking to two leading Luftwaffe aces during the Battle of Britain. Name the two aces.

45. Which British port became known as 'Hellfire Corner' during the summer of 1940? Clue: it could also be a type of 'sole'.

46. A German He 111 bomber is pictured flying over the Isle of Dogs in London at the start of the Luftwaffe's evening raids on 7 September 1940. Why was this date significant?

47. The date 15 September 1940 is now celebrated as Battle of Britain day. Why is this?

48. What was the name of the controversial tactic of sending mass fighter formations up against the Germans?
A) The Super Wing B) The Mass Wing C) The Big Wing.

49. Complete the next line of this speech by Winston Churchill in 1940: 'The gratitude of every home in our Island, in our Empire, and indeed throughout the world, except in the abodes of the guilty, goes out to the British airmen who, undaunted by odds, unwearied in their constant challenge and mortal danger, are turning the tide of the world war by their prowess and by their devotion.'

50. Which British designer was responsible for the development of the Hurricane aircraft? *Came my dyns.*

51. Truth or fiction? After 7 September 1940, London was bombed by the Germans for 100 consecutive nights.

52. What was the name of the German bombing campaign against British cities between September 1940 and May 1941?

53. What is the estimated number of civilians killed during the bombing of British cities between 1940 and 1941?
A) 5,500   B) 13,500   C) 43,500.

54. The remains of this British cathedral following an air attack on the night of 14 November 1940 can still be seen. What city is it?

55. After London and Liverpool, which British city was the next most heavily bombed?
A) Bristol   B) Southampton   C) Birmingham.

56. Truth or fiction? The German secret weapon *Knickebein*, which translates as 'crooked leg', was a bomb that changed direction at the last minute.

57. Which London Underground station was closed permanently to be used as an air raid shelter?
A) Aldwych   B) Bethnal Green   C) Elephant and Castle.

58. Which type of air raid shelter, consisting of two curved corrugated sheets of steel, was buried 1.2 metres (4 ft) into the ground? *Trades horse lenn.*

59. Indoor 'kit' shelters were named after which British minister?
A) Henderson Shelter   B) Morrison Shelter   C) Shackleton Shelter.

60. More than 100 people died when a German bomb struck which Underground station in January 1941? Clue: it's a type of institution.

61. What item is pictured here?

62. On 27 September 1940, Japan signed which treaty in Berlin?

63. What was formed in 1940 by the British to help foreign resistance fighters within occupied Europe?
A) MI9   B) SOE   C) MI7.

64. Which country did Italy invade in 1940?

65. By the end of October 1940, there were some 3,000 UXBs in Britain. What does UXB mean?

66. The WVS provided services such as serving refreshments from mobile canteens during the bombing of Britain. What did WVS stand for?

67. Which gallantry medal was established in Britain to reward those civilians showing outstanding bravery away from the fighting front line?

68. Truth or fiction? Despite weighing just 1 to 2 kilograms (2 to 4 lbs), the thermite charge of a German incendiary bomb could create fires hot enough to melt steel.

69. In 1940, rationing was initially set up in Britain for which foods?
A) Butter and sugar   B) Butter, sugar, bacon and ham
C) Tea and biscuits.

70. Truth or fiction? In wartime Britain, bread was never rationed.

71. Which British government ministry was created to help with wartime shortages and was led by Lord Woolton? *Miffy into doors.*

72. Although fruit and vegetables were not rationed in wartime Britain, shortages still led to a campaign for civilians to grow their own. What was this campaign known as?

73. Truth or fiction? In June 1940, Britain developed a plan to invade Ireland?

74. As wartime shortages developed in Britain, clothing rationing led the government to develop which thrifty campaign? Clue: repairs were the name of the game.

75. What nickname, derived from the British Minister of Labour at the time, was given to conscripts between the ages of 18 and 24 who were deployed as miners in the coal mining industry?

76. In March 1941, which US Act allowed Britain to borrow war supplies on the promise of a later repayment? *Deals leen*.

77. Name this British aircraft, which was used to attack the Italian navy whilst it was at anchor in November 1940.

78. After the failure of the bombing campaign against Britain, Germany focused on which method of warfare to try to knock Britain out of the war?

79. What did German U-boat crews call the period 1940–41, when they sunk a large tonnage of Allied shipping in the Atlantic? A) Easy Time B) Leisure Time C) Happy Time.

80. Which Italian naval base was attacked on 11 November 1940 by British torpedo bombers?
A) Bari B) Taranto C) Brindisi.

81. What was Turkey's status for most of the war until February 1945?

82. What was the nickname of the popular all-in-one suit, which could be pulled over clothing quickly during an air raid, and which was a favourite of Winston Churchill? Clue: you wouldn't hear anyone wailing whilst wearing this!

83. Truth or fiction? In 1940, Hitler postponed a planned invasion of Switzerland in order to concentrate on the invasion of Britain?

84. Which inflatable object was tethered to the ground and used to force enemy bombers to fly higher and be less accurate? *Ball range or boa.*

85. In autumn 1940, Hitler sent troops to Romania principally to secure which vital oilfield?

86. What was Plan Dog and what did it signify? Clue: it was American.

87. Which German fighter, with a maximum range of 1,150 km (715 miles) and elliptical wings, was put forward as a potential fighter for the Luftwaffe, but lost out to the ME 109 before the war?

88. Set up in Canada, which Allied scheme was designed to train pilots for future air combat?

89. Britain proposed to expand its army to 55 divisions. How many of these divisions were expected to come from the British Empire and its dominions?
A) 5   B) 15   C) 21.

90. Britain created units in 1940 that were designed to resist should there be an invasion. What were these units called?
A) Auxiliary units   B) Resistance units   C) Covert units.

91. Which British organization arranged the evacuation of children to Australia, Canada, New Zealand and South Africa.

92. A British policeman can be seen helping evacuees at a railway station. Why did the British government fail to evacuate every child from British cities?

93. What was the unpleasant-looking British cartoon character created to highlight shoppers wasting money?
A) Wasteful Bug   B) Squander Bug   C) Fritter Bug.

94. What was the British mission to the US in 1940 that shared emerging new technology, including research on jet engines, the feasibility of an atomic bomb and the cavity magnetron?

95. What was the nickname of William Joyce, a Nazi radio propagandist, who at times was said to have up to half of the British public tuning in to his broadcasts?

96. Which neutral European country offered safe transit for refugees from all over the continent?
A) Switzerland   B) Spain   C) Portugal.

97. Which type of cargo ship, mass-produced in the United States, delivered vital resources to Britain?
A) Independence ships   B) Liberty ships   C) Freedom ships.

98. What nickname was given to German U-boat groups which emerged in October 1940 to attack Atlantic convoys? Clue: this could be during a howling gale.

99. In September 1940, Italy attacked British and Commonwealth forces in which country?
A) Greece   B) Albania   C) Egypt.

100. Who was British commander in the Middle East in the autumn of 1940? *Bad call have wirl*

101. Which British artist and sculptor produced a series of drawings of people in air raid shelters during the Blitz?

ANSWERS

1. Sculptor Arno Breker, and architects Albert Speer and Hermann Giesler.

2. B) Romania.

3. This was the attack by the British on French warships at Mers-el-Kébir, near Oran in North Africa. It prevented the French ships from falling into German hands and convinced many that Britain would fight on.

4. RDF or 'Range and Direction Finding'.

5. Sir James Sommerville.

6. B) 'Führer weather'. Most of the early victory parades were often blessed with lovely weather, hence the phrase.

7. The Supermarine Spitfire.

8. R. J. Mitchell.

9. Truth. But there were still sufficient numbers for it to play a key role in the Battle of Britain.

10. Elliptical wings.

11. RAF Duxford in Cambridgeshire, now Imperial War Museum Duxford.

12. C) Emil.

13. B) Luftwaffe.

14. Fiction. The ME 109 could only sustain 30 minutes over England despite being based just across the Channel.

15. Hermann Göring.

16. It directed British planes straight to the oncoming enemy aircraft, rather than dispersing them on unnecessary patrols.

17. Truth. The problem prior to battle was a lack of trained pilots.

18. *Kanalkampf* or 'Channel Battle'.

19. C) Ventnor. The Germans thought the raid was ineffectual and decided attacks on radar stations would be of little use.

20. RAF Manston in Kent.

21. Hurricane. These were the most numerous of the British fighters.

22. A) Flying Pencil.

23. New Zealand.

24. B) Finger Four.

25. *Adlerangriff* or 'Eagle Attack'.

26. B) *Adlertag* or 'Eagle Day'.

27. Black Thursday.

28. Paul Nash. The painting is in the collection of Imperial War Museums.

29. Truth. By the time a vehicle came to collect him he had beaten his opponents!

30. 'Scramble'.

31. Sir Hugh Dowding.

32. Operation Sealion.

33. B) Bentley Priory.

34. Women's Auxiliary Air Force.

35. C) He was the highest scoring Allied pilot.

36. 303 (Polish) Fighter Squadron.

37. Sir Quintin Brand.

38. Fiction. They had a range of 129 km (80 miles) from the coast.

39. The Observer Corps.

40. The Home Guard.

41. A) The British Indian Army.

42. Ireland and the United States.

43. C) The Hardest Day.

44. Major Werner Mölders (left) and Major Adolf Galland (right).

45. Dover.

46. It was a change in German tactics. The Luftwaffe believed they had successfully damaged the RAF, so began to bomb London instead of RAF targets. Heavy bombing of the capital allowed the RAF to regroup, and this is often seen as the turning point of the Battle of Britain.

47. The fighting on this day led to large German losses, which meant Germany did not achieve air superiority to support the launch of an invasion.

48. C) The Big Wing. This tactic was not favoured by Dowding due to the time it took to assemble the aircraft in the air.

49. 'Never in the field of human conflict was so much owed by so many to so few.'

50. Sydney Camm.

51. Fiction. London was bombed on 57 consecutive nights.

52. The Blitz.

53. C) 43,500.

54. Coventry.

55. C) Birmingham.

56. Fiction. It was radio beams, directed from stations in Europe, which directed the German aircraft to targets.

57. A) Aldwych. It was used as a shelter for artworks from London museums and galleries.

58. Anderson Shelter.

59. B) Morrison Shelter, named after Herbert Morrison.

60. Bank station.

61. A Morrison shelter, set up in a dining room, in 1941.

62. The Tripartite Pact with Germany and Italy.

63. B) SOE or Special Operations Executive.

64. Greece.

65. Unexploded bomb.

66. Women's Voluntary Service.

67. The George Cross. The majority of initial awards were for bomb disposal or search and rescue during the Blitz.

68. Truth. A single plane would carry hundreds of these types of incendiary bombs.

69. B) Butter, sugar, bacon and ham.

70. Truth. However, the government-mandated National Loaf was an unpopular, peculiar grey colour.

71. Ministry of Food.

72. Dig for Victory.

73. Truth.

74. Make Do and Mend.

75. Bevin Boys.

76. Lend Lease.

77. Fairey Swordfish.

78. Restricting the flow of resources into Britain using U-boats to sink shipping.

79. C) Happy Time.

80. B) Taranto.

81. Neutral. Turkey declared war on Germany in 1945 in order to attend the first meeting of the United Nations. The Allies required that all participants should actively oppose Hitler.

82. The 'siren suit'.

83. Truth.

84. Barrage balloon.

85. The oilfields of Ploesti.

86. This was a memorandum regarding what strategy the US would pursue in the event of entering the war. Of the four scenarios named A to D, D was an offensive war in the Atlantic and a defensive war in the Pacific, leading to the US strategy of 'Germany first'.

87. Heinkel HE 112.

88. Empire Air Training Scheme.

89. C) 21. A division could be anywhere between 10,000 and 20,000 men, so this was around 400,000 troops.

90. A) Auxiliary units. Britain was the only country at that point to set up a resistance network prior to any actual invasion.

91. Children's Overseas Reception Board.

92. Evacuation was only voluntary. Many children remained, often to support families.

93. B) Squander Bug.

94. The Tizard Mission.

95. Lord Haw Haw.

96. C) Portugal.

97. B) Liberty ships.

98. Wolfpacks.

99. C) Egypt.

100. Archibald Wavell.

101. Henry Moore.

CHAPTER 4

Heading South and East

1. Operation Compass took place in North Africa in 1940–41. What was it?

2. Which German commander arrived in Tripoli on 12 February 1941 to take charge of the German *Afrika Korps*?

3. The insignia for the German *Afrika Korps* in North Africa featured which plant?
   A) Coconut   B) Palm tree   C) Desert flower.

4. Truth or fiction? Three men were required to operate the German Enigma machine during World War II.

5. What six-letter cipher text, sent out every day at 6:05 a.m., was a word which helped to break the German Enigma naval codes?

6. How many ways could a German Enigma machine code a message?   A) 10,000 million million
   B) 100,000 million million   C) 1 million million.

7. What did Winston Churchill refer to as 'The geese that laid the golden eggs and never cackled'?

8. What codename was given to the German Enigma messages deciphered by British codebreakers?

9. Which British mathematician was a leading codebreaker at Bletchley Park? *Gain tan rul.*

10. The British battlecruiser HMS *Hood* was sunk by which German ship in the Denmark Strait in May 1941?

11. How many crew survived out of 1,418 sailors on HMS *Hood* when it was sunk in May 1941? A) None B) One C) Three.

12. How many Italian troops surrendered to the British at Bardia in January 1941? A) 10,000 B) 26,000 C) 36,000.

13. Name this Libyan port, besieged by the Germans in 1941?

14. After the mass surrender of Italian forces in North Africa, British troops were deployed to which country in 1941? Clue: this turned out to be a classic mistake.

15. What nickname was given to the commander of the *Afrika Korps*, due to his skill at conducting warfare in the desert?

16. Which Middle Eastern country was occupied by British forces in June 1941?
A) Iran   B) Iraq   C) Syria.

17. Operation Mercury, in May 1941, was the codename given to the German airborne invasion of which island in the Mediterranean?

18. Yugoslavian leader Prince Paul joined the Axis powers in March 1941. What happened next?

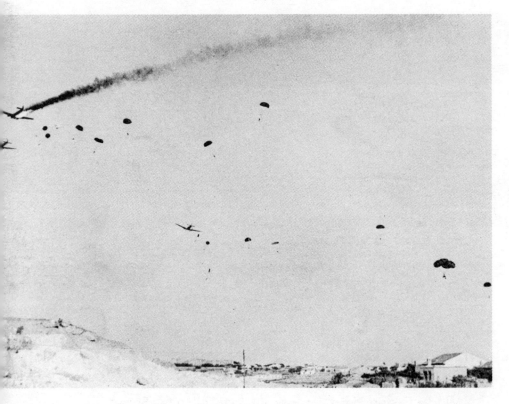

19. German parachutists can be seen landing on Crete in May 1941. What targets did the German troops aim to capture to aid their supply?

20. Which airfield in Crete was captured by German paratroopers? *Me lame*

21. Name this German artillery gun which played a major role with all German forces in the war.

22. In August 1941, British and Soviet forces occupied which Middle Eastern country to secure supplies to the Soviet Union? A) Iraq B) Syria C) Iran.

23. What was Operation Exporter? Clue: it was an Allied invasion.

24. The Yugoslavian communist partisan leader, Josip Broz, is better known by what other name?

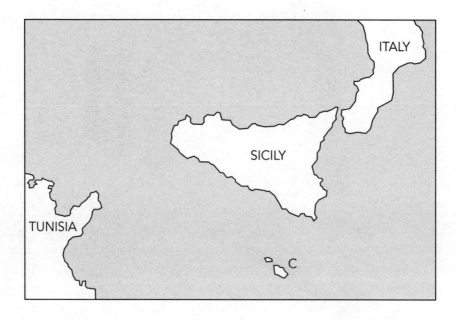

25. Which Mediterranean island (C) enabled the Allies to harass German re-supply convoys to North Africa?

26. Which European capital fell to German forces on 27 April 1941?
A) Belgrade   B) Athens   C) Sarajevo.

27. A significant five-year neutrality agreement was signed by which two nations on 13 April 1941, allowing both countries to fight on only one front?

28. Operation Barbarossa was the German invasion of the Soviet Union. When did it begin?

29. Operation Retribution was a German operation in 1941, part of the opening phase of the German invasion of which country?

30. This photo shows the wreckage of a German Messerschmitt which crashed in Scotland on 10 May 1941. Who was on board?

31. Truth or fiction? The German ambassador in Moscow warned the Soviet Union of an impending attack in 1941.

32. What was the name of the Nazi secret plan that called for any territories captured in the east to be 'Germanized', and which would lead to the ethnic cleansing of the local Slavic populations?

33. On 6 June 1941, German armed forces issued the Commissar Order. What was this order?

34. What name was given to Hitler's headquarters near Rastenburg in East Prussia? *Sow ar fill.*

35. 'We have only to kick in the door and the whole rotten edifice will come crashing down.' Who said this, and what were they referring to?

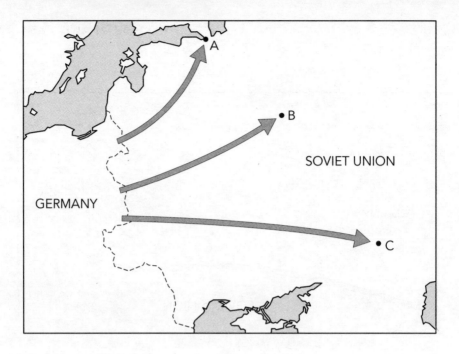

36. Which Soviet cities (A and B) were the main targets for the advancing German forces in 1941?

37. What was the Nazi plan to divert supplies from Soviet people to the German invasion forces on Soviet territory?
A) The Food Plan   B) The Living Plan   C) The Hunger Plan.

38. During planning for the invasion of the Soviet Union, German military called for an occupation up to the 'A–A Line'. Between which two places was this?

39. How many German armies were used to attack the Soviet Union and in what direction were they to advance?

40. Truth or fiction? One month after the start of Operation Barbarossa, German forces had captured territory three times the size of Germany.

41. On 23 June 1941, Stalin set up his supreme headquarters, giving it which old Tsarist title? *Ask vat.*

42. How many horses were used by the German army for the invasion of the Soviet Union?
A) 225,000   B) 425,000   C) 600,000.

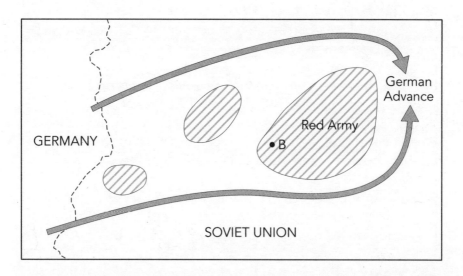

43. Which Soviet city, (B), was captured by German forces on 26 June 1941, following the encirclement of mass formations of Red Army troops?

44. Captured motor transport from which defeated country was used to bolster the German invasion of the Soviet Union? A) Poland   B) France   C) Norway.

45. Which Soviet commander took over from General Pavlov following the Soviet collapse in the summer of 1941? *Mine to shok.*

46. The USSR had more than 10,000 tanks at the start of the war, but what type of tanks made up the bulk of Soviet tank formations?

47. Which Soviet tank was first encountered by German forces during the invasion of the Soviet Union? Clue: it was named after the year its basic design was first conceived.

48. What was the name of Soviet battalions which were used as cannon fodder in an attempt to halt German advances? A) The People's Army   B) The Soviet Volunteers C) The People's Militia.

49. The encirclement of a large number of Soviet troops during Operation Barbarossa in the summer of 1941 was known by the Germans as what?

50. Which German encirclement of Soviet troops on 28 June 1941 trapped over 400,000 men? *Tibs lay ok.*

51. In which area were Soviet troops encircled by German Army Group South on 2 August 1941?

52. On 16 September 1941, in the largest military encirclement in history, German forces trapped more than 700,000 Soviet troops to the east of which city?   A) Kharkov   B) Minsk   C) Kiev.

53. What was the German *Einsatzgruppen*, which operated on the Eastern Front in 1941, having first been used in Poland?

54. What is the name of the ravine near Kiev where more than 30,000 Jews were killed by the Germans in September 1941?

55. In this photo, German troops occupy a burning Russian village. What type of infrastructure did the Soviets evacuate east to deny to the advancing Germans in 1941?
A) Food supplies   B) Factories and industrial equipment
C) Agricultural tools.

56. The United States occupied which Atlantic island on 7 July 1941. Clue: they needed warm clothes.

57. Name this German machine gun, used extensively by German forces after 1942.

58. In this photo, Franklin D. Roosevelt and Winston Churchill are seated on the quarterdeck of HMS *Prince of Wales*. What document did they sign during this meeting from 9 to 12 August 1941?

59. Which four principles, put forward by Franklin D. Roosevelt during his meeting with Churchill in Newfoundland in 1941, went on to form the Universal Declaration of Human Rights?

60. Which city (A) in the Soviet Union was cut off from the rest of the country by advancing German forces in 1941, with lake (B) becoming its only supply route?

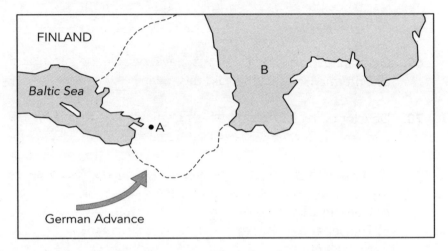

61. Nicknamed *Mosinka* by troops, which rifle was standard issue for the Soviets during the German invasion?

62. Truth or fiction? Stalin's own son was captured by German forces in one of the large encirclement battles of 1941.

63. The internal law agency of the Soviet Union, the People's Commissariat for Internal Affairs, was known by what abbreviation? A) Spetzna B) Smersh C) NKVD.

64. On 8 September 1941, German forces captured the town of Shlisselburg, beginning their siege of which city?
A) Stalingrad B) Kiev C) Leningrad.

65. What were used for the first time on 3 September 1941, by testing a new substance on Soviet and Polish prisoners?

66. Truth or fiction? On 8 September 1941, German bombers targeted hospitals in the city of Leningrad.

67. Which major tactical change by the Germans during Operation Barbarossa began on 12 August 1941?

68. What name was given to Russian troops who formed into resistance bands after being left behind the front line?
A) Bandits B) Partisans C) Guerrillas.

69. German leaders referred to the Slavic people they occupied as *Untermenschen*. What did this mean?

70. Developed by IG Farben, which pesticide was tested for the first time in September 1941 on humans?

71. On 26 July 1941, Britain and the United States froze the assets of Japan in retaliation for what?
A) Conscription in Japan
B) The Japanese occupation of French Indochina
C) Japan's neutrality pact with the Soviet Union.

72. What was the nickname of the volunteer American pilots who flew with the Chinese in 1941 and whose planes had distinctive nose art? Clue: these animals weren't meant to fly.

73. Operation Typhoon began in October 1941. What was it?

74. The Germans were greatly hampered by *rasputitsa* in Russia. What was this? A) The Soviet rocket system
B) Torrential autumnal rains   C) Arctic wind.

75. How many days did the siege of Leningrad last?
A) 500 B) 900 C) 1,000.

76. Truth or fiction? German panzers reached Orel, south of Moscow, but senior Soviet officers did not believe it had happened despite panzers passing trams in the streets.

77. What is the surname of the Soviet commander of the Reserve Front near Vyazma in October 1941? *Don y buny.*

78. What Soviet weapon, that German troops called 'Stalin's organ', first appeared during the Battle of Moscow?

79. On 15 October 1941, Stalin decided to evacuate the Soviet government from Moscow to which city?
A) Kuibyshev   B) Nizhny Novgorod   C) Perm.

80. Which Soviet agent in Tokyo informed Stalin that Japan was about to strike against the United States? *Gods hire crar.*

81. By the end of November 1941, how close were the German troops to the centre of Moscow?
A) 29 km (18 miles)   B) 39 km (24 miles)   C) 14 km (9 miles).

82. What lake near Leningrad was used to supply the city during its siege, especially when it froze in winter? *Doll aka age.*

83. Truth or fiction? Soviet aircraft flew in sub-zero temperatures during the Battle of Moscow because they had skis rather than wheels to land on.

84. What name was given to the supply route over the frozen lake near the besieged city of Leningrad?
A) Road of Bones   B) Road of Food   C) Road of Life.

85. Which war minister became prime minister of Japan on 18 October 1941? *Dote hi koji.*

86. What did Germans collect to send to troops on the Eastern front as the winter worsened in 1941?
A) Stoves   B) Gloves   C) Coats.

87. In August 1941, the US embargoed what commodity to Japan, accelerating Japan's decision to go to war?

88. In this photo, Soviet troops dressed in white launch a counterattack against German soldiers. When did the Soviet Union launch its surprise counteroffensive outside Moscow?

89. What action did Hitler take in response to the German retreat from Moscow in 1941?

90. Operation Crusader was an operation to do what in 1941?

91. Australian troops can be seen sheltering in caves from an air raid in the Libyan port of Tobruk. What nickname was given to those trapped at Tobruk?

92. What was the name of Himmler's deputy who led the Reich Security Main Office? *Chiney air herd rdh.*

93. What was the name of the German conference in early 1942 which saw the Nazis set out plans for the extermination of the Jews of Europe?

94. Operation Hercules was a cancelled plan to do what? Clue: it involved a stubborn island in the Mediterranean.

95. What nickname was given to soldiers of the British Eighth Army who fought in North Africa?

96. Which wartime song first became popular during the desert campaign? A) 'White Cliffs of Dover' B) 'Lili Marlene' C) 'Tuxedo Junction'.

97. Which British magician was responsible for developing camouflage which magically transformed trucks into tanks, as seen in this photo?
A) Jasper Lynne B) Jasper Maskelyne C) James Maskell.

98. British troops in North Africa inspect two tanks. In the background is a Matilda tank, but which US-manufactured tank can be seen in the foreground?

99. What was used by the Italians on 19 December 1941 in the harbour of Alexandria in Egypt?
A) Human torpedo   B) Diver mine   C) Snorkel mine.

100. Truth or fiction? Malta was so heavily bombed between 1941 and 1942 that the whole island was awarded the Victoria Cross, the highest medal of valour.

ANSWERS

1. An Allied Western desert offensive, which led to the surrender of the Libyan port of Tobruk to Allied forces.

2. Erwin Rommel.

3. B) Palm tree.

4. Truth. One man worked the machine, another called out encrypted messages, while a third man wrote the message.

5. *Wetter*, German for 'weather', announcing the daily forecast.

6. A) 10,000 million million.

7. The codebreakers based at Bletchley Park in Britain.

8. Ultra.

9. Alan Turing.

10. *Bismarck*.

11. C) Three.

12. C) 36,000.

13. Tobruk, besieged between April and December 1941.

14. Greece. Rommel pushed the Allies back across Libya to the Egyptian border as a result of the troop deployments to Greece.

15. The 'Desert Fox'.

16. B) Iraq.

17. Crete.

18. He was overthrown in a coup, which hastened a German invasion of Yugoslavia.

19. They aimed to capture key airfields on Crete.

20. Maleme.

21. 88mm artillery gun.

22. C) Iran.

23. This was the occupation of Syria by Allied troops, due to the Vichy French authorities allowing German aircraft to use bases there.

24. Tito.

25. Malta.

26. B) Athens.

27. The Soviet Union and Japan. It secured both countries' 'back doors', allowing the Soviets to turn to the growing threat of a German invasion, and the Japanese to concentrate on Pacific expansion and conflict with the US.

28. 22 June 1941.

29. Yugoslavia. This operation was the bombing of Belgrade.

30. Deputy Führer, Rudolf Hess. He had flown to Britain to try to arrange a peace deal with Britain prior to the German invasion of the Soviet Union. Parts of the plane are now in the collection of Imperial War Museums.

31. Truth. Anti-Nazi Ambassador Schulenburg warned the Soviets, but Stalin ignored the warning thinking it was German misinformation.

32. *Generalplan Ost* or General Plan East.

33. The Commissar Order was for German forces to execute as partisans any political officers they captured.

34. Wolf's Lair.

35. Hitler said this to his commanders when referring to the Red Army and the invasion of the USSR.

36. Leningrad (A) and Moscow (B).

37. C) The Hunger Plan. This led to the deaths of millions in Nazi-occupied Soviet territories.

38. Archangel in northern Russia and Astrakhan on the Caspian Sea, placing the bulk of the Soviet population and industry in German hands if the invasion was successful.

39. Three army groups. Army Group North attacked towards Leningrad, Army Group Centre towards Moscow and Army Group South towards Ukraine.

40. Fiction. German forces had captured territory roughly double the size of Germany.

41. *Stavka*.

42. C) 600,000.

43. Minsk.

44. B) France.

45. Marshal Timoshenko.

46. Obsolete T-26 tanks and BT light tanks.

47. The T-34, invented in 1934.

48. C) The People's Militia.

49. *Kesselschlacht* ('Cauldron Battle').

50. Bialystok.

51. Uman.

52. C) Kiev.

53. Mobile groups of SS, including the security service and police, which followed the advancing German army and were responsible for killing Jews, political leaders, intellectuals and anyone who was perceived as a threat to German authority.

54. Babi Yar.

55. B) Factories and industrial equipment. Some 2,500 industrial enterprises were shipped east to the Urals.

56. Iceland.

57. MG42. It was often called 'Spandau' by the British.

58. The Atlantic Charter.

59. Freedom from fear, freedom from want, freedom to worship and freedom of speech.

60. Leningrad was supplied across (B) Lake Ladoga.

61. The Mosin-Nagant rifle.

62. Truth. Stalin was unsympathetic, declaring in private he wished his son had not been born. Lieutenant Yakov Dzhugashvili died in 1945, when he was shot having thrown himself against barbed wire at his internment camp.

63. C) NKVD.

64. C) Leningrad.

65. The gas chambers at Auschwitz.

66. Fiction. The bombers targeted food depots, destroying six months' worth of food, with tragic future consequences for the population of the city.

67. Hitler ordered Army Group Centre to divert its tank force to help Army Group South in the Ukraine.

68. B) Partisans.

69. Sub-humans.

70. Zyklon-B, used in the gas chambers of extermination camps.

71. B) The Japanese occupation of French Indochina.

72. The Flying Tigers.

73. A German assault on Moscow.

74. B) Torrential autumnal rains. The mud on the mainly unsurfaced Russian roads hindered German vehicles.

75. B) 900 days. It was lifted on 27 January 1944.

76. Truth. Leading panzers reached Orel where the trams were still running.

77. Budyonny.

78. The Katyusha rocket launcher.

79. A) Kuibyshev.

80. Richard Sorge. He provided the information which allowed the Soviets to transfer large formations of troops from Siberia to help in the defence of Moscow.

81. A) 29 km (18 miles).

82. Lake Ladoga.

83. Fiction. Soviet aircraft had lubricants for operating in low temperatures, giving air superiority to the Soviets.

84. C) Road of Life.

85. Tojo Hideki.

86. C) Coats.

87. Oil.

88. 5 December 1941.

89. Hitler dismissed the Army commander in chief, making himself responsible for all future military decisions.

90. To relieve the port of Tobruk.

91. The Rats of Tobruk.

92. Reinhard Heydrich.

93. The Wannsee Conference.

94. A cancelled German and Italian plan to invade Malta.

95. The Desert Rats.

96. B) 'Lili Marlene'.

97. B) Jasper Maskelyne.

98. M3 Stuart Tank.

99. A) Human torpedo.

100. Fiction. The island was awarded the George Cross.

CHAPTER 5

Widening World War

1. Who was the Emperor of Japan in December 1941 who approved orders for attacks on US, British and Dutch interests in the Pacific and Southeast Asia? *Thor ohii.*

2. Which Japanese admiral planned the surprise attack on the US naval base in Hawaii?
    A) Yamaha   B) Motoyama   C) Yamamoto.

3. Name the US naval base on the Hawaiian Island of Oahu.

4. Called 'a date that would live in infamy', when was the surprise attack on the United States in Hawaii?

5. Where did the Japanese fleet set sail from on 26 November 1941 to attack the US?
    A) Hokkaido   B) Kurile Islands   C) Honshu.

6. Truth or fiction? US pilots Kenneth M. Taylor and George Welch were sleeping after a Christmas party when they heard explosions at their base, and took to the air still wearing their tuxedos from the night before.

7. To counteract a trade embargo, Japan planned to attack the resources of the Dutch East Indies in 1941. What was the name of this plan?
    A) The Southern Plan   B) The Eastern Plan
    C) The Western Plan.

8. In this photograph, a distant view of the attack on the US base in Hawaii, which US battleship (centre) can be seen in a plume of black smoke having just exploded?

9. Which naval formation greatly assisted the Japanese pilots when they attacked ships in Hawaii?

10. Which US warship capsized during the Japanese attack on Hawaii? *Shook mal sua.*

11. How many people were killed by the Japanese attack on Hawaii in 1941?   A) 1,403   B) 2,403   C) 3,403.

12. Truth or fiction? US forces were put on a state of high alert for a Japanese attack on Hawaii.

13. Which Japanese commander led the first wave of planes that attacked Hawaii?

14. What codeword was used by Japanese planes to confirm that complete surprise had been achieved with the attack on Hawaii?

15. Which aircraft carrier served as a flagship for Admiral Nagumo during the attack on Hawaii in 1941?
A) *Akagi* B) *Soryu* C) *Ugo*.

16. Following the US declaration of war on Japan, which country also declared war on the US on 11 December 1941?

17. Which US air base was attacked during the Japanese bombing of Oahu in December 1941? *Feel hide werl.*

18. What did US intelligence services call their intercepts of Japanese diplomatic signal traffic?
A) Rising Sun B) Torch C) Magic.

19. Truth or fiction? President Roosevelt decided the day before the Japanese attack on Hawaii to press ahead with research on an atomic weapon.

20. A *hachimaki* was worn by Japanese pilots as they prepared to attack. What was it?
A) A white headband with a red 'rising sun' on it
B) A red 'rising sun' on a white arm band
C) A flying jacket with a red 'rising sun' on its pocket.

21. Which Japanese fighter plane was nicknamed 'Zeke' by the Allies and first entered service in 1940?

22. What do IJN and IJA stand for?

23. How many Japanese aircraft carriers took part in the attack on Hawaii?
A) Four B) Five C) Six.

24. What type of ships were absent from Hawaii when the Japanese attacked in 1941?

25. Which British battleship, pictured, was sunk off the coast of Malaya by Japanese aircraft in 1941?

26. Which British battlecruiser was sunk off Malaya in December 1941? *Mules sherp.*

27. Operation Drumbeat was also called the 'Second Happy Time'. What was it?

28. Which British colony surrendered to the Japanese on Christmas Day, 1941?

29. What type of lightly armoured tank proved a vital part of early Japanese victories in the Pacific?
A) Type 95 Tank   B) Type 100 Tank   C) 'Aichi' Tank.

30. Truth or fiction? Due to the use of bicycles by Japanese forces on the Malay Peninsula, the advance on Singapore became known as the 'Bicycle War'.

31. Who was in command of the Japanese forces during the invasion of Malaya in late 1941?

32. Where did the Japanese establish a landing on the north-east coast of Malaya in 1941? *Bark to hua.*

33. This photo shows a coastal defence gun at Singapore. Why were these guns unsuccessful in defending Singapore from Japanese invasion?

34. Singapore surrendered to the Japanese on 15 February 1942. How many British and Commonwealth troops were captured when the city fell?
A) 20,000   B) 60,000   C) 80,000.

35. Which British general surrendered Singapore to the Japanese and went on to spend the rest of the war as a prisoner in Manchuria?

36. Truth or fiction? Major-General Henry Gordon Bennett, commander of the Australian Eighth Division at Singapore, escaped on a *sampan*.

37. Which strait, separating Singapore from the Malayan mainland, was successfully crossed by the Japanese in early 1942? *The raj is root.*

38. What landed for the first time in Britain on 26 January 1942?   A) Sherman tanks   B) US troops   C) Hershey bars.

39. Which island, across the Strait of Malacca from Singapore, was invaded by Japanese troops on 14 February 1942?
A) Bali B) Sumatra C) Goa.

40. Which key target was secured by Japanese parachutists near Palembang in February 1942? Clue: this had been under embargo.

41. What name has been given to the defeat of a combined Allied naval squadron off the Dutch East Indies by the Japanese on 27 February 1942?
A) The Battle of the Indian Ocean
B) The Battle of Australian Bight C) The Battle of Java Sea.

42. Name this US general who commanded in the Pacific south-west throughout World War II?

43. Which US possession was attacked by Japanese troops on 8 December 1941? *Hit pips in helep.*

44. Which peninsula (B) and fortress island (C) in Manila Bay are shown in the map below?

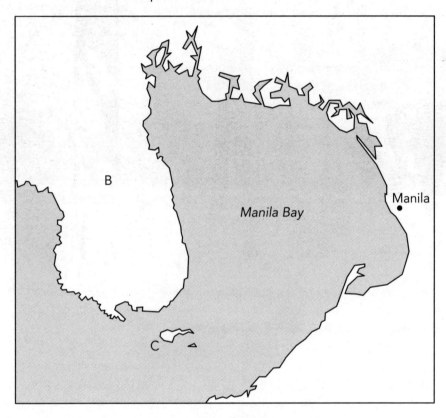

45. Truth or fiction? When Japanese planes bombed Manila in 1941, the local population were unsure what to do and sheltered under trees for protection.

46. In this photo, American prisoners of war on Luzon are marched into captivity in 1942. The tropical conditions and brutality of the Japanese meant many died on the march. What did the march become known as?

47. Which Pacific island was attacked by the Japanese on 8 December 1941, surrendering on 23 December? Clue: you can sometimes be left behind in this!

48. Which fortress island in Manila Bay finally surrendered to the Japanese in 1942? *Cried or gor.*

49. Which country did the Japanese invade on 23 December 1941 in order to disrupt supplies to Chinese Nationalists and gain access to natural resources such as rubber?

50. What is the name of the Philippines peninsula to which US troops withdrew, where they held out until April 1942?

51. What was the nickname of US Major General Joseph Stilwell who led Chinese Nationalist troops into Southeast Asia to help British forces?
A) Salt Joe   B) Vinegar Joe   C) Ketchup Joe.

52. After abandoning Rangoon in early 1942, British troops retreated to the border with India. What was significant about this retreat?

53. Following an order by President Roosevelt, General MacArthur left Manila and evacuated to which country?
A) New Zealand   B) New Guinea   C) Australia.

54. What name did the Japanese give to their vast conquered area of Southeast Asia, where they intended to lead other nations in removing Western influences?

55. Which Communist guerilla leader received Allied support in his fight against the Japanese in Indo-China? *Mihin hoch.*

56. In the photo below, a B-25 bomber takes off bound for a daring raid on Tokyo on 18 April 1942. Named after its commander, what was the raid called?

57. Which US aircraft carrier launched B-25 bombers for a bombing raid on Tokyo in 1942?

58. The attack by B-25 bombers from a US aircraft carrier on Tokyo was morale-boosting for the US. How far were the bombers from Tokyo when they launched?
A) 563 km (350 miles)   B) 805 km (500 miles)
C) 1,046 km (650 miles).

59. What name was given to the gap in the Japanese defensive perimeter from where an aircraft carrier launched the Tokyo raid in 1942?

60. What name was given to the naval battle between US and Japanese aircraft carriers east of New Guinea on 7 May 1942?   A) The Battle of Java Sea
B) The Battle of the Coral Sea   C) The Battle of Pearl Sea.

61. Which US aircraft carrier was attacked by Japanese dive bombers off New Guinea, and was later abandoned and sank? *Losing Ext Sun.*

62. What did the Allies call the Japanese Aichi D3A dive bomber?

63. Although the naval action at New Guinea in May 1942 was a tactical victory for Japan, what did it prevent the Japanese from doing following the clash?

64. Which US Pacific island base (B) was attacked by Japanese forces in June 1942?

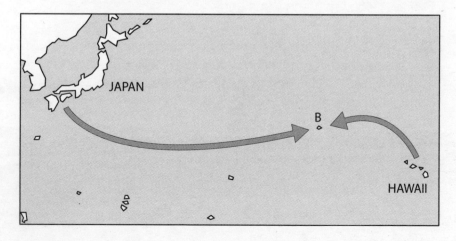

65. Which US dive bomber sank more shipping than any other US plane in the Pacific?
A) F4U Vought Corsair   B) Grumman F8F Bearcat
C) Douglas SBD Dauntless.

66. Truth or fiction? The naval battle at New Guinea in 1942 was the first time that aircraft carriers had fought each other, but both naval forces could still see the enemy ships on the horizon.

67. Which US carrier was heavily damaged off New Guinea in 1942, but was repaired in Hawaii in just 45 hours?

68. Which four Japanese aircraft carriers launched an airstrike on Midway in June 1942?
A) *Kaga, Akagi, Soryu* and *Hiryu*
B) *Akagi, Soryu, Nagumo* and *Kaga*
C) *Kaga, Akagi, Soryu* and *Mikuma*.

69. Which Japanese admiral commanded aircraft carriers at the Battle of Midway?

70. Which ship was part of the US force which assembled north-east of Midway to surprise the Japanese? *Presents us ire.*

71. Although the US lost 300 sailors and airmen at the Battle of Midway, what were the estimated losses for the Japanese?
A) 1,500   B) 2,500   C) 3,500.

72. Task One, allocated when areas of command were established in the Pacific in July 1942, asked the US Navy to do what?   A) Defend Midway   B) Blockade New Guinea
C) Capture Guadalcanal.

73. Which naval battle occurred on 8–9 August 1942 in the Solomon Islands, leading to a defeat for the Allies?

74. What was the name given by US sailors to the nightly Japanese convoys that brought reinforcements to the Solomon Islands? A) Tokyo Express B) Solomon Sprint C) Pacific Promenade.

75. Where was Henderson Field, named after a US Marine killed at Midway, and fiercely fought over by US and Japanese troops?

76. The US carrier USS *Hornet* was sunk in October 1942 during which Pacific naval battle? A) The Battle of Santa Cruz B) The Battle of Coral Sea C) The Battle of Midway.

77. Which Australian town was attacked by Japanese aircraft on 19 February 1942?

78. Which part of the Solomon Islands chain was captured by US Marines on 7 August 1942? *Can dual gala.*

79. On 22 July 1942, Japanese forces landed at Buna and Gona on which Pacific island?
A) Australia B) New Guinea C) Borneo.

80. Which mountainous jungle trail in Papua was fought over by Japanese and Australian troops throughout July and August 1942? *Took lark ida.*

81. Executive order 9066 was passed in the US in February 1942. What did it allow the US Army to do?

82. How many ethnic Japanese were estimated to live on the West Coast of America in early 1942?
A) 90,000 B) 120,000 C) 240,000.

83. Truth or fiction? Following the Japanese attack on Hawaii, all ethnic Japanese living on the US West Coast were forced to sell their property and businesses and were sent to internment camps.

84. With production soaring during the war, what did Roosevelt call the wartime US economy?

85. US women served in the WASP. What did the acronym stand for and what did the women do?

86. What name was given to the poster of a female US war worker, used to recruit women to work?
A) Wanda the Welder   B) Rosie the Riveter
C) Mabel the Machinist.

87. What vital 'area denial' weapon was used substantially in the desert campaign in North Africa?

88. Who (pictured) took over command of the British Eighth Army in August 1942?

89. What did soldiers serving on both sides in the desert believe was their biggest 'enemy'?
A) Heat   B) Flies   C) Lack of water.

90. Name the Egyptian railway halt where British forces held the advance of German troops in July 1942?

91. Which area of salt marsh concentrated the fighting in North Africa to a narrow coastal strip?

92. How few German supply ships reached their destination in the Mediterranean due to the Germans failure to capture Malta?   A) One in three   B) One in four   C) One in six.

93. Name this British armoured car, used extensively throughout the desert war.

94. What key logistical problem faced the Germans during the fighting in Egypt in 1942?

95. How did Montgomery change the desert campaign for Britain when he took over in 1942?

96. The photograph shows British and Commonwealth forces training intensively in minefield clearance. How deep were German minefields in Egypt at El Alamein?

97. Operation Lightfoot took place in the North African desert in 1942. What was it?

98. Name the two types of tanks that can be seen in this photo.

99. What ailment meant Rommel missed the start of the fighting in Egypt in October 1942?
A) Stomach complaint   B) Stress   C) Heat exhaustion.

100. What three main phases were planned for Allied forces during the Battle of El Alamein in October 1942?

101. Truth or fiction? For the first time since the Battle of Britain, church bells were rung across Britain after victory at El Alamein in 1942.

102. Complete this line from a speech by Winston Churchill on 10 November 1942: 'Now this is not the end. It is not even the beginning of the end ...' (Reproduced with the permission of Curtis Brown, London, on behalf of the Estate of Winston S. Churchill, ©The Estate of Winston S. Churchill)

ANSWERS

1. Hirohito.

2. C) Yamamoto.

3. Pearl Harbor.

4. 7 December 1941.

5. B) Kurile Islands.

6. Truth. They shot down several Japanese planes and both received the Distinguished Service Cross.

7. A) The Southern Plan.

8. USS *Arizona*.

9. The American battleships were lined up together in a 'Battleship Row'.

10. USS *Oklahoma*.

11. B) 2,403.

12. Fiction. On the Sunday morning of the attack many sailors were on shore leave.

13. Mitsuo Fuchida.

14. *Tora, Tora, Tora. Tora* translates as 'tiger', and it was a simple codeword which could be quickly transmitted.

15. A) *Akagi*.

16. Germany.

17. Wheeler Field.

18. C) Magic.

19. Truth. The decision was taken on 6 December 1941.

20. A) A white headband with a red 'rising sun' on the forehead.

21. The Mitsubishi A6M Zero.

22. Imperial Japanese Navy and Imperial Japanese Army.

23. C) Six.

24. Aircraft carriers.

25. HMS *Prince of Wales.*

26. HMS *Repulse.*

27. German U-boat attacks on Allied shipping off the eastern coast of the US in January 1942.

28. Hong Kong.

29. A) Type 95 Tank.

30. Fiction. The Japanese did use fast-moving, bicycle-mounted infantry, but the name is not true.

31. Lieutenant General Yamashita.

32. Khota Baru.

33. The coastal batteries could be turned to fire on the Malay peninsula but the guns only had armour-piercing shells designed to hit ships, and not high explosive shells, which would have been more effective against land-based troops.

34. C) 80,000.

35. General Arthur Percival.

36. Truth.

37. Johore Strait.

38. B) US troops.

39. B) Sumatra.

40. The Royal Dutch Shell oil refineries at Pladjoe.

41. C) The Battle of Java Sea.

42. General Douglas MacArthur.

43. The Philippines.

44. Bataan peninsula (B) and Corregidor Island (C).

45. Truth. An American marine claimed to see women shelter under trees, with some opening umbrellas for extra protection.

46. The Bataan Death March.

47. Wake Island.

48. Corregidor.

49. Burma.

50. Bataan, on the island of Luzon.

51. B) 'Vinegar Joe', due to his alleged caustic personality.

52. It was the longest retreat in British military history, around 966 km (600 miles) in nine weeks.

53. C) Australia.

54. The Greater East Asia Co-Prosperity Sphere.

55. Ho Chi Minh.

56. The 'Doolittle Raid', named after Lieutenant-Colonel James H. Doolittle.

57. USS *Hornet*.

58. C) 1,046 km (650 miles). The aircraft had been stripped to lighten them for the distance, but many did not reach landing strips in China after bombing Tokyo.

59. The 'Midway Keyhole'.

60. B) The Battle of the Coral Sea.

61. USS *Lexington*.

62. The Aichi 'Val'.

63. The Japanese were forced to abandon their attack on Port Moresby, which would have isolated Australia from the US.

64. Midway.

65. C) Douglas SBD Dauntless.

66. Fiction. It was the first time that two sides had fought a naval battle without seeing each other, with a distance between each fleet of 322 km (200 miles).

67. USS *Yorktown*. The Japanese believed the carrier had been sunk at 'Coral Sea', which convinced them to press on with their attack on Midway.

68. A) *Kaga*, *Akagi*, *Soryu* and *Hiryu*.

69. Admiral Nagumo.

70. USS *Enterprise*.

71. C) 3,500 men.

72. C) Capture Guadalcanal where the Japanese were building an airfield.

73. The Battle of Savo Island.

74. A) 'Tokyo Express'.

75. Guadalcanal.

76. A) The Battle of Santa Cruz.

77. Darwin.

78. Guadalcanal.

79. B) New Guinea.

80. Kokoda Trail or Kokoda Track.

81. It allowed the army to remove ethnic Japanese Americans from areas deemed vulnerable to Japanese attack.

82. B) 120,000.

83. Truth. Some protested unsuccessfully through US courts.

84. The 'arsenal of democracy'.

85. Women's Airforce Service Pilots. They ferried aircraft from factories to air bases.

86. B) Rosie the Riveter. Wanda the Welder and Mabel the Machinist were also used, but Rosie the Riveter has become iconic.

87. Landmines and minefields.

88. Bernard Montgomery.

89. B) Flies.

90. El Alamein.

91. The Qattara Depression.

92. B) One in four.

93. Humber (Mk II) armoured car.

94. German supply lines were long, extending some 1,931 km (1,200 miles) back to Tripoli.

95. He designed coordinated battle plans and determined that the Allies would only fight when they had enough equipment. Although this had been tried under previous British commanders, Montgomery developed the Eighth Army into a cohesive, capable and confident fighting formation which had been lacking previously in the desert campaign.

96. The minefields were 8 km (5 miles) deep.

97. The operation was an all-arms phase, including artillery, infantry and tanks, to clear German minefields, ready for the next part of the Battle of El Alamein.

98. Grant and Lee tanks.

99. A) Stomach complaint. He returned to Africa on 26 October 1942.

100. 'Break-in', 'Dogfight' and 'Break-out'.

101. Fiction. Church bells were silenced across the country in 1940 following the evacuation from Dunkirk, and were only to be rung to warn of invasion. For the first time since the ban, they were rung to celebrate the victory of El Alamein.

102. 'But it is, perhaps, the end of the beginning.'

CHAPTER 6

Turning Points

1. What was the popular nickname of the Russian factory complex at Chelyabinsk in the Urals?
   A) Aviograd   B) Tankograd   C) Spetznagrad.

2. What was Operation Sledgehammer, an Allied operation that was cancelled? Clue: the objective featured in a much later campaign.

3. German forces captured which Soviet port on 4 July 1942?

4. What was the nickname of the 800mm railway gun which was used in Crimea by German forces in 1942?
   A) Friedrich   B) Gustav   C) Henri.

5. What was the German offensive Operation *Blau* ('Blue')?

6. Who was the Soviet commander of the south-west front in 1942? *So tank helms rai hom.*

7. What was the name of the Soviet salient that was cut off in May 1942, when more than 250,000 Red Army troops were captured?

8. Truth or fiction? The Soviet evacuation from the Crimea in 1942 became known as 'Dunkirkograd'.

9. Named after two key rivers, what was the corridor through which German forces attacked south-west into Russia in June 1942?

10. Which Soviet city was captured by the German First Panzer Army on 23 July 1942? *To rovs.*

11. Which oil field did German forces reach in the summer of 1942, only to find that the facilities had been destroyed by retreating Soviet troops?   A) Maikop   B) Maksim   C) Misha.

12. Who commanded the German Sixth Army in south-west USSR in 1942? *Rich fud as purile.*

13. In this photo, German troops advance towards a smoking Soviet city in 1942. What is the name of this city, which would become a pivotal battle of World War II?

14. Soviet Order No. 227 was issued on 28 July 1942 and was entitled *Ni shagu nazad*. What did this mean? Clue: this was a line in the sand.

15. Where did Operation Jubilee, a disastrous raid on 19 August 1942, take place?

16. German forces advance on the Soviet city of Stalingrad. The city sits on the banks of which river (A)?

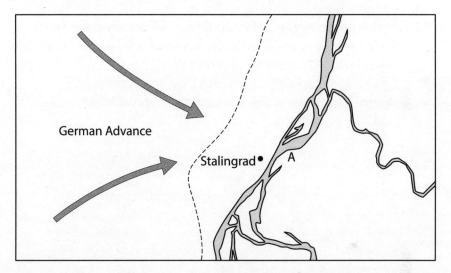

17. Name the key strategic summit, a burial mound, found in the city of Stalingrad?

18. What was the name of the Soviet sniper who became famous in Stalingrad, and was later depicted in the feature film *Enemy at the Gates*?

19. What was the name of Hitler's headquarters that was set up outside Vinnytsia in the Ukraine in 1942?
A) Werwolf   B) Condor   C) Führerbunker.

20. Which mountain, the highest in the Caucasus, was scaled by German troops on 21 August 1942?
A) Mount Aragats   B) Mount Kazbek   C) Mount Elbrus.

21. Who was the chief Soviet political officer at Stalingrad? *This cake ivh rhukn.*

22. From which country were the troops defending the rear of German forces at Stalingrad?
A) Norway   B) Romania   C) Spain.

23. What was Operation Uranus, a decisive Soviet operation?

24. Intended to be a diversion to distract other German forces from supporting Army Group South, what name did the Russians give to their operation in late 1942 near Rzhev?

25. Operation Ironclad was a British plan to seize the port of Diego Suarez. On which island in the Indian Ocean is this port?

26. Truth or fiction? The attack by a Japanese midget submarine in the harbour of Diego Suarez was the only direct military support Germany received from its ally during the war.

27. Soviet Intelligence believed they had trapped 86,000 men at Stalingrad, but how many Axis troops were actually trapped in the city by November 1942?
A) 90,000   B) 190,000   C) 290,000.

28. Truth or fiction? During German air supply operations to troops in the Stalingrad encirclement, Hermann Göring could not be contacted because he had retired to a Parisian hotel.

29. What was *Wasserzuppe*, eaten by the German Sixth Army cut off at Stalingrad?
A) Snow mixed with cabbages
B) Snow mixed with pieces of dog meat
C) Snow mixed with pieces of horse meat.

30. Which German airfield was used to supply troops trapped at Stalingrad? *Tank is a stay.*

31. What did Hitler ban in his headquarters out of respect for the Sixth Army trapped at Stalingrad?
A) Bread and wine   B) Brandy and champagne
C) Cigarettes and beer.

32. To what position did Hitler promote the commander of the German Sixth Army at Stalingrad, in the expectation that he would commit suicide rather than surrender?

33. What was Operation Winter Storm? Clue: it failed to storm the Soviet lines.

34. On 27 January 1943, what did the US launch? Clue: these were in broad daylight.

35. Name the US bomber, pictured, which spearheaded the US bombing campaign over Europe?

36. Operation Torch was which Allied operation in 1942?

37. How many task forces were involved in the Allied landings in north-west Africa in 1942?   A) One   B) Three   C) Five.

38. At which three locations did Allied troops land in north-west Africa in 1942?

39. In this photo, US troops can be seen landing in Africa. Which port in Algeria was defended by Vichy French forces, leading to some Allied casualties?

40. Which Vichy French high commissioner was detained by the Allies after ordering a ceasefire on 9 November 1942? *Maid lard an lar.*

41. What was the German plan *Fall Anton* or 'Operation Anton' in 1942?

42. Following Allied landings in Morocco and Algeria, which German commander was responsible for sending troops to Tunisia? *Berater less glink.*

43. Truth or fiction? Following the occupation of southern France by German forces, Hitler also ordered German troops into the Pyrenees in 1942.

44. In this photo, troops and ammunition are being brought ashore from LCAs in Algeria in November 1942. What did LCA stand for?

45. Name this American general, pictured here at the ceremonial opening of the Allied North African Headquarters in Algiers?

46. Which African city was captured by the British Eighth Army on 23 January 1943?
A) Algiers   B) Tunis   C) Tripoli.

47. Which German defensive line was located at the base of the Bay of Gabes in Tunisia? *Rate him len.*

48. Who did Mussolini sack following the loss of Libya to the Allies in early 1943?

49. Which German general fought alongside Rommel in the Tunisian desert in 1943?

50. Where was the narrow pass in Tunisia where Rommel attacked US troops in February 1943? *Pains ass seekr.*

51. Which US commander was put in overall command of the Allies in North Africa in late 1942?

52. Name this fearsome German tank which was introduced in Russia and Tunisia in 1942–3?

53. Where did Operation *Ochsenkopf* or 'Ox Head', a German operation in 1943, take place?
A) Libya   B) Morocco   C) Tunisia.

54. Name the North African capital (B) which was captured by the Allies on 7 May 1943?

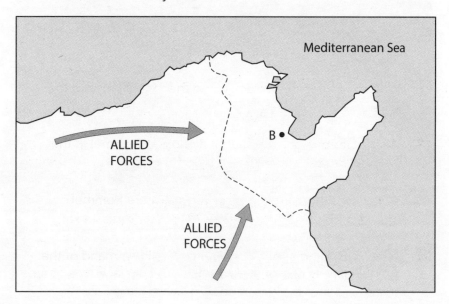

55. The German *Wehrmacht* general staff had the initials OKW. What did this abbreviation mean?

56. Formed in 1940, which British desert specialists had the initials LRDG and a nickname 'Libyan Desert Taxi Service'?

57. What British special forces unit, pictured here, was formed in 1941 and famously raided Axis airfields in the North African desert?

58. Nicknamed the 'Phantom Major', which British soldier was the founder of one of the most famous special forces groups to come out of the desert conflict? *Vads lit riding.*

59. Which army group was set up by the Germans fighting the Allies in Tunisia in 1943? A) Army of Tunisia B) Army of the Desert C) Army of Africa.

60. Which German commander, injured by Allied aircraft in the hand and eye in Tunisia, would later try to play a pivotal role in the war against Hitler?

61. What did WDAF, the Allied Air Force in the desert campaign in North Africa, stand for? A) Wings Desert Air Force B) Wadi Air Force C) Western Desert Air Force.

62. On 18 April 1943, one British and four American squadrons of fighters shot down 74 German aircraft over Tunisia. What nickname was given to this day?

63. How many Axis forces were captured after Tunis fell to the Allies on 7 May 1943? A) 100,000 B) 200,000 C) 250,000.

64. Which commander first took command of US II Corps in Tunisia? Clue: there was a popular film made about him.

65. Which Japanese commander was shot down during Operation Vengeance in April 1943?

66. Which German admiral became head of the German Navy in 1943? *Möan air lizt dd*

67. Which naval battle gained crucial significance for the Allies in 1943 and why?

68. Truth or fiction? Allied analysis showed that German U-boats generally sunk the same number of ships in every attack they launched.

69. Which new weapon, with 24 mortars launched from Allied warships, was used for the first time during the Battle of the Atlantic in 1943? A) Depth Charge B) Grey Wolf C) Hedgehog.

70. What was a Leigh Light and what role did it play in the Battle of the Atlantic?

71. In what month in 1943 did the Allies lose fewer ships in the Atlantic than the Germans did submarines?
A) February   B) May   C) June.

72. What did the initials SOE for a British secret organization stand for?
A) Secret Operations Executive
B) Special Operations Executive
C) Secret Occupation Executive.

73. Which British colonel led the British SOE in World War II?
Coin bugs nilb.

74. What was the target of Operations Grouse, Freshman and Gunnerside in occupied Norway?

75. What name was given to a French paramilitary force set up in January 1943 and led by Joseph Darnand?

76. What was Operation North Pole, a successful German operation which was also known as *Englandspiel*?

77. Which prominent Nazi was attacked by two Czech volunteers on 27 May 1942?

78. Named after a district in Norway, what name was given to the 1965 British war movie about SOE operations in Norway?

79. The Secret Army (*Armée secrète*) was an underground movement in which occupied country?
A) France   B) Belgium   C) Both France and Belgium.

80. What was the name of the stadium in Paris where Parisian Jews were held in the summer of 1942, prior to being transported 'east'?

81. The *Milorg* was the underground army in which occupied European country?

82. Named 'Shark' by British codebreakers at Bletchley Park, what development was introduced in February 1942 to Enigma machines?

83. The picture above shows a Cockle Mk II canoe used by a ten-man British team to attack shipping at Bordeaux in December 1942. What name was given to the men who took part in this hazardous raid?

84. A Hawker Sea Hurricane Mark I can be seen on board a CAM ship, SS *Empire Darwin*. These ships were used in the Atlantic and Arctic to protect convoys. What did CAM stand for?

85. Operation Frankton was which Allied raid?

86. Truth or fiction? Pilots who flew planes from CAM ships in convoys had special hooks attached to their flight suits, allowing them to snag onto ships' wires when parachuting out over the convoy.

87. Nicknamed the 'Digger's Darling', which Australian light machine gun was ideal for jungle fighting?

88. Which two Russian ports received the bulk of supplies from Arctic convoys between 1941 and 1943?

89. Which two-letter initial was given to eastbound Atlantic convoys heading to the UK during World War II?
A) NY   B) BO   C) HX.

90. Operation Jupiter in 1942 was an Allied plan that never happened. Where was it going to invade?

91. Name the US flying boat that played a major role throughout World War II, especially in support of naval convoys.

92. What name was given to U-boats designed for refuelling other U-boats at sea? They were introduced to extend a U-boat's operational time.

93. What was fitted to German submarines during World War II that allowed them to remain submerged for long periods of time? Clue: this could also be used by a casual diver.

94. What is the name of these German aircraft, pictured opposite, which played a vital role in the Battle of the Atlantic in co-ordination with German submarines?

95. What was the name of the US amphibious vehicle which played an important role in Europe and the Pacific? Clue: let's hope its feathers are waterproof.

96. Which British commander led long-range penetration operations behind Japanese lines in Burma? *Town rage eid.*

97. The EAM–EALS guerilla movement operated in which occupied European country?
A) Yugoslavia   B) Czechoslovakia   C) Greece.

98. British MI9 and US MIS-X were secret movements principally tasked with what role?

99. What British special forces unit operated behind Japanese lines in Burma? *This dinc.*

100. In case they were left behind enemy lines, what item was issued to Allied pilots or commandos embarking on raids? Clue: it was made of a delicate fabric.

ANSWERS

1. B) Tankograd.

2. An Allied plan to attack the Cotentin peninsula in France.

3. Sevastopol.

4. B) Gustav.

5. An operation to strike south-west to the Soviet oil fields in the Caucasus.

6. Marshal Timoshenko.

7. Izyum salient.

8. Fiction. Troops were taken out by small boats in a Dunkirk-style 'miracle', but the name is fictitious.

9. Don–Donets corridor.

10. Rostov.

11. A) Maikop.

12. Friedrich Paulus.

13. Stalingrad. A pall of smoke is hanging over the city as German infantry move into the outskirts.

14. 'Not one step back'.

15. Dieppe in France. Canadian forces suffered heavy casualties during the raid on the port. The lessons learned would inform Allied planning for the future invasion of France.

16. River Volga.

17. Mamayev Kurgan.

18. Vasily Zaitsev.

19. A) *Werwolf* ('Werewolf').

20. C) Mount Elbrus, at 5,642 m (18,510 ft) high.

21. Nikita Khrushchev.

22. B) Romania.

23. An attack on the German flanks in November 1942 around Stalingrad, intending to encircle German forces.

24. Operation Mars.

25. Madagascar

26. Truth. It was the only direct military support Japan offered Germany.

27. C) 290,000.

28. Truth. Göring was in the Ritz hotel in Paris, whilst the resupply by air at Stalingrad was proving woefully insufficient.

29. C) Snow mixed with pieces of horse meat.

30. Tatsinskaya.

31. B) Brandy and champagne.

32. Field Marshal. Despite the promotion Paulus surrendered on 31 January 1943.

33. This was the German attempt to relieve the trapped army at Stalingrad.

34. US bombing raids on Germany.

35. B-17 'Flying Fortress'.

36. An Allied landing in which 100,000 troops came ashore in north-west Africa.

37. B) Three task forces: the US western, central and eastern task forces.

38. Casablanca, Oran and Algiers.

39. Oran. American troops can be seen on board a landing craft going in to land there.

40. Admiral Darlan.

41. This was the German occupation of Vichy France in response to Allied landings in north-west Africa.

42. Albert Kesselring.

43. Truth. Spain ordered a partial mobilization to counter the threat.

44. Landing Craft Assault.

45. General Mark Clark.

46. C) Tripoli.

47. Mareth Line.

48. Count Ciano, his foreign minister and son-in-law.

49. General Hans von Arnim with his Fifth Panzer Army.

50. Kasserine Pass.

51. General Dwight D. Eisenhower.

52. Tiger tank. This Tiger I tank was captured by British forces in Tunisia, 1943.

53. C) This was a limited German action in Tunisia, in early spring 1943.

54. Tunis.

55. *Oberkommando der Wehrmacht* or 'Supreme Command of the Armed Forces'.

56. The Long Range Desert Group.

57. The Special Air Service (SAS).

58. David Stirling.

59. C) Army of Africa.

60. Claus von Stauffenberg.

61. C) Western Desert Air Force.

62. The 'Palm Sunday Massacre'.

63. C) 250,000. Many were Italian troops.

64. George Patton.

65. Admiral Yamamoto, planner of the Pearl Harbor attack.

66. Admiral Dönitz.

67. The Battle of the Atlantic. Allied war aims were dependent on being able to move men and resources safely between the US and Britain.

68. Truth. This led the Allies to increase the overall size of Atlantic convoys whilst losses remained the same.

69. C) Hedgehog. The mortars exploded on contact rather than at a set depth and it became a decisive weapon in the Battle of the Atlantic.

70. The Leigh Light was an aerial searchlight used in conjunction with airborne radar. This meant that long-range planes could target German submarines which were travelling at night on the surface.

71. B) May. The German crews called it 'Black May' when a fifth of the entire German U-boat fleet was lost.

72. B) Special Operations Executive.

73. Colin Gubbins.

74. The Norsk Hydro Plant at Vemork, used to create 'heavy water' for the German nuclear programme.

75. *Milice française.*

76. This was a German counter-intelligence operation against Allied agents operating in the Netherlands, which led to the capture of some 50 agents.

77. Reinhard Heydrich. Although the wounds he sustained in the attack were not fatal, he died a few days later from septicaemia, leading to savage reprisals against the Czechs.

78. *The Heroes of Telemark.*

79. C) Both France and Belgium.

80. The *Vélodrome d'Hiver.*

81. Norway.

82. A fourth rotor was added to German naval Enigma machines.

83. The Cockleshell Heroes.

84. Catapult Armed Merchantman.

85. The British commando 'Cockleshell Heroes' raid on shipping in the occupied French port of Bordeaux in 1942.

86. Fiction. The only way for a pilot to be rescued was by boat, which was especially hazardous in freezing waters.

87. The Owen Gun.

88. Murmansk and Archangel.

89. C) HX. These originated in Halifax, Nova Scotia and left from New York via Halifax once the US entered the war.

90. Northern Norway.

91. The Consolidated PBY Catalina.

92. *Milchkühe* or 'Milk Cows'. They were used to refuel and re-arm other U-boats at sea.

93. A *schnorchel* or 'snorkel'. It was a pipe which could reach the surface when at periscope depth.

94. Focke-Wulf Fw 200C Condors.

95. DUKW or 'Duck'.

96. Orde Wingate.

97. C) Greece.

98. They were responsible for facilitating the escape of Allied prisoners of war and for helping those trying to evade capture behind enemy lines, such as aircrew.

99. Chindits.

100. Silk escape maps. They survived harsh treatment, including immersion in water, and were easy to conceal.

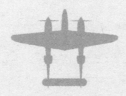

CHAPTER 7

Supreme Leaders

1. What name was given to the coalition of Great Britain, the United States and USSR?   A) The Triple Entente B) The Grand Alliance   C) The Super Powers.

2. Churchill, Roosevelt and Stalin met together only twice during World War II. Where did these meetings take place and in what years?

3. Stalin, Roosevelt and Churchill sit on the veranda of the Soviet Legation in November 1943. What nickname did the leaders have when they were together?

4. What sword, being shown here to President Roosevelt, with Churchill and Stalin looking on, was a gift to the Soviet leader from Churchill?

5. How many countries signed up to the 1942 Declaration of the United Nations to continue the fight against the Axis powers and not negotiate a separate peace?
A) 26 B) 46 C) 56.

6. Which conference took place between Roosevelt and Churchill at the Anfa Hotel in January 1943?

7. Truth or fiction? At a conference in January 1943, Stalin was invited to join Roosevelt and Churchill but declined because he did not like the location.

8. Codenamed Quadrant, where did an Anglo–American meeting take place in August 1943?
A) Montreal   B) Quebec   C) New York.

9. What key strategic decision did Churchill and the British persuade the US to adopt at a conference in January 1943?

10. At the Anglo–American conference in January 1943, what did President Roosevelt demand of Allied policy?
A) To bomb Germany into submission
B) To support the USSR
C) An invasion of Europe and the complete unconditional surrender of Nazi Germany and Japan.

11. Truth or fiction? President Roosevelt believed in face-to-face meetings so much that he became the first US president to leave his country during wartime.

12. Winston Churchill and Franklin D. Roosevelt sit talking in January 1943. Which two French commanders did Churchill persuade Roosevelt to bring together in front of the press at this conference?

13. Truth or fiction? The Soviet Operation Spark in January 1943 tested a new type of bomb.

14. Which Soviet city was abandoned by German forces in February 1943, only to be re-taken the following month?

15. What did British Bomber Command gain approval for in February 1942?

16. Who was the head of British Bomber Command from February 1942? *Shirt arr ruah.*

17. British bombers fought the Battle of the Ruhr in 1943. What nickname did Allied crews give the Ruhr Valley at this time? A) Death Valley   B) Happy Valley   C) Blind Valley.

18. The German city of Hamburg was bombed on 27 July 1943. What did the bombing raid unleash?

19. Who said about the bombing of Germany: 'They sowed the wind, and now they are going to reap the whirlwind'?

20. Name this bomber, which was a key part of the British bombing campaign over Germany?

21. How many tonnes of bombs were dropped by the Allies over Europe during World War II?   A) 1 million tonnes   B) 2.7 million tonnes   C) 6.4 million tonnes.

22. What metal structures were found on many air bases in England and were often used to house aircrews? *Sent is shun.*

23. Named after British towns, which three heavy bombers began to replace the Hampden and Wellington bombers in 1943?

24. What was significant about the British air raid against the German city of Cologne on 30 May 1942?

25. Which aircraft flew in advance of night bombers during air raids and marked target areas with incendiary bombs?   A) Lighters   B) Way markers   C) Pathfinders.

26. Named after a travel guide, which German air raids were launched against historic cities in England in 1943? *Reek said beard.*

27. Launched on 16 May 1943, what were the main targets for one of the most famous British air raids of the war?

28. Which key US innovation was supposed to provide pin-point bombing accuracy by day? *Moon sign bet drbh.*

29. Which raid by USAAF bombers took place on a major ball-bearing plant and Messerschmitt factory, and which led to heavy US losses?

30. What name was given to strips of aluminium foil dropped by Allied bombers to confuse German radar?   A) Sheet lightning   B) Silver ghost   C) Window.

31. What nickname was given to the US B-17 bomber which was equipped with ten machine guns and four gunners?

32. Which colonel arrived in Britain with the US 305 Bomb Group? *Mist lace ruy.*

33. Which Hollywood actor flew with the US Eighth Air Force on five combat missions from England during 1943?
A) Ronald Reagan   B) Clark Gable   C) James Stewart.

34. What was the Allied air operation Tidal Wave?

35. What nickname was given to red and green marker flares dropped over Germany, usually in the first wave of air raids?
A) Fairy lights   B) Christmas trees   C) Star bursts.

36. Truth or fiction? The German flak tower found in Berlin's Tiergarten district was named the 'Lion' flak tower.

37. Why were air raid sirens in Berlin given the nickname 'Meyer's trumpet'?

38. What name was given to Jews who were living in secrecy in Berlin during the war? *Rinse a mubs.*

39. What nickname was given to the upward-firing cannons used by German night fighters against Allied bombers? Clue: this was darkly out of tune.

40. Who was the designer of the British 'bouncing bomb'? *Warns is label.*

41. Who said, 'Germany is a fortress, but it is a fortress without a roof'?

42. How many US airmen were estimated to have been killed or captured during the bomber offensive in Europe?
A) 10,000   B) 30,000   C) 50,000.

43. Germany operated two types of prisoner of war camps, Oflags and Stalags. What was the main difference between the two types?

44. Name the medieval castle in Saxony which was supposed to be escape-proof?

45. Which type of vehicle was found in the attic of a castle prison camp in Saxony when it was liberated by US troops? A) Hot air balloon B) Glider C) Light aircraft.

46. A rope of bed linen hangs on the west front of the guardhouse after Polish Army officers had been caught in mid-air trying to escape from Oflag IV-C. What nickname did prisoners at this camp give to successful escape attempts?

47. What was prized by Allied prisoners of war in Europe, helping many to stave off malnutrition?

48. Franz von Werra is the only known Axis prisoner of war to achieve what?   A) He escaped from a gulag in Siberia B) He escaped from Canada C) He escaped from North Africa via Gibraltar.

49. Which document was signed by nations agreeing to treat prisoners of war humanely? *Gone venc innovate.*

50. Which Pacific coral atoll was attacked by the US Second Marine division in November 1943?

51. What do the initials LVT stand for as a type of vehicle used by US Marines in the Pacific?   A) Landing Vehicle Tank B) Landing Vehicle Titan   C) Landing Vehicle Tracked.

52. Which coral atoll in the Gilbert Islands was attacked by the US 27th Infantry Division on 20 November 1943?

53. Which two lines of advance in the Pacific were determined at a conference in Washington in May 1943?

54. Which key location in New Guinea was reinforced by Japan, but bypassed by US forces? *Bal a ru.*

55. What name was given to the battle which took place off Lau, New Guinea, in 1943, and saw the destruction of Japanese troop transports?   A) The Battle of Bismarck Sea B) The Battle of Coral Sea   C) The Battle of Lau.

56. Which low-level bombing technique, which involved aircraft dropping bombs just short of a ship's side, was used effectively by the US Fifth Air Force in the Pacific? A) Bounce bombing   B) Skip bombing   C) Short bombing.

57. Which US admiral was commander in chief in the South West Pacific theatre? *Mall way slihie.*

58. Operation Cartwheel was an advance in the Pacific aimed at neutralizing which Japanese base?

59. Which future US president was run down by a Japanese destroyer whilst commanding PT109 in the Pacific?

60. As a result of heavy losses in the battle for New Georgia in the Solomon Islands, what change of strategy did US commanders adopt?

61. What was the nickname of US Naval Construction Battalions in the Pacific? Clue: it came from the initials.

62. Truth or fiction? The main priority for Allied forces whenever a Pacific island was captured was to build an airstrip.

63. Name this US fighter with 'gull-wings', a key weapon in the Pacific theatre?

64. Why were few Japanese troops taken captive during the battle of Tarawa in 1943?
A) There were fewer troops on the atoll than thought
B) There were only construction workers
C) Japanese troops ended the battle in a mass suicide charge.

65. Which key battle in the Soviet Union in 1943 is named after location C?

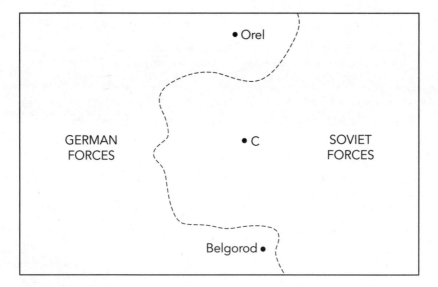

66. What was the objective of the German plan Operation Citadel or *Zitadelle* in the spring of 1943?

67. What name was given to this type of German tank, which was one reason why Hitler delayed attacking in Russia in 1943, as he waited for them to become available?

68. Which Soviet ground attack aircraft fought in the skies above Kursk in 1943? *Must or kiv.*

69. On which date did German forces begin their attack at Kursk?   A) 5 May 1943   B) 5 June 1943   C) 5 July 1943.

70. Which German rocket launcher was used during the Battle of Kursk? *Fern bew reel.*

71. Which flank of the German attack was concentrated at its strongest on the Soviet salient at Kursk?

72. Which Soviet and German tank armies engaged in battle on 12 July 1943 at Kursk?

73. Where did a major armoured battle during the Kursk campaign take place in the summer of 1943? *Hoop ork vark.*

74. Operation Kutuzov was a Soviet attack in July 1943 to take back which city?
A) Stalingrad   B) Minsk   C) Orel.

75. How many lines of defence did the Red Army manage to construct in the Kursk salient prior to the battle in 1943?
A) Two B)   Eight   C) Sixteen.

76. What codeword was used by Soviet commanders to signal their tanks to attack German panzers during the Battle of Kursk?   A) *Ivan*   B) *Stal*   C) *Nyet.*

77. What tactic did Soviet tanks use with their greater numbers against the more heavily armed German tanks during the Battle of Kursk?

78. How many mines were estimated to have been laid by the Red Army in their defensive lines in the Kursk salient by 1943?   A) 100,000   B) 1 million   C) 5 million.

79. Truth or fiction? Despite victory at the Battle of Kursk, the Red Army lost more men and tanks than the Germans.

80. Which two Soviet cities were liberated by the Red Army following the successful defence of the Kursk salient in the summer of 1943?

81. Which leading German panzer ace took command of a Tiger tank platoon during the Battle of Kursk? *Team what in milc.*

82. Operation Husky was the Allied invasion of which island in 1943?

83. What was Churchill referring to when he said there was a 'soft underbelly of Europe'?

84. Which two commanders were given command of the US and British armies for the invasion of Sicily, despite alleged friction between the pair?

85. Truth or fiction? The Allied invasion of Sicily was on such a scale that it was comparable in size to the invasion of northern France the following year.

86. What was the Allied Operation Mincemeat?

87. Truth or fiction? In order to deceive the Germans, the Allies disguised the body of a tramp who had died from rat poison as a British officer carrying secret plans, and let the Germans find the washed-up body with the fake plans.

88. What was the name of the book and film released in the 1950s which depicted the military deception by the Allies in the Mediterranean in 1943?
A) *The Man in the Sea*
B) *The Man Who Never Was*
C) *The Man Who Wasn't Real.*

89. British and US troops link up in Sicily, at a road junction outside Randazzo. Which two armies were used by the Allies for the invasion of Sicily?

90. Which Sicilian port was quickly captured on the first day of the Allied invasion of Sicily? *Cray uses.*

91. When did the Allies land troops for the invasion of Sicily?
A) 10 June 1943   B) 10 July 1943   C) 10 August 1943.

92. Instructions are being signalled to waiting LCI landing craft on the opening day of the invasion of Sicily. What does LCI stand for?

93. Truth or fiction? During the Allied invasion of Sicily, the local mafia refused to help US troops and were loyal to Mussolini.

94. Which German panzer division attacked the US landings in Sicily near Gela?

95. What was the nickname of the US 1st Infantry Division which landed in Sicily in the summer of 1943?
A) The Big One
B) The Big Red One
C) The Big Red.

96. Which Italian general and politician took over following the arrest of Mussolini in 1943? *Great boil do poi.*

97. Which Sicilian town was the main port through which 100,000 Axis soldiers escaped across to Italy?
A) Syracuse
B) Catania
C) Messina.

98. Truth or fiction? US General Patton was almost court-martialled for striking a soldier from the US 1st Division whilst visiting a field hospital in Sicily in August 1943.

99. Mussolini was detained in a hotel in which town in the Apennines following his arrest by Italian authorities in 1943?

100. Which German commander led a raid to rescue Mussolini from Italian captivity in September 1943?

101. On which day did the Italian government sign an armistice with the Allies?
A) 1 September 1943
B) 3 September 1943
C) 6 September 1943.

ANSWERS

1. B) The Grand Alliance.

2. Tehran in 1943 and Yalta in 1945.

3. The Big Three.

4. The 'Sword of Stalingrad', a gift from British King George VI to the defenders of Stalingrad.

5. A) 26.

6. The Casablanca Conference.

7. Fiction. Stalin felt he could not leave Russia whilst the Red Army was engaged at Stalingrad.

8. B) Quebec, Canada.

9. To abandon an attempted invasion of France until at least spring 1944.

10. C) An invasion of Europe and the complete unconditional surrender of Nazi Germany and Japan.

11. Truth. He travelled widely to attend conferences during the war.

12. General Charles de Gaulle and General Henri Giraud.

13. Fiction. It aimed to end the German siege of Leningrad.

14. Kharkov.

15. Area bombing. The twin aims were to destroy vital infrastructure and civilian morale.

16. Arthur Harris.

17. B) 'Happy Valley'.

18. A firestorm, which killed 42,000 civilians. Temperatures reached 1,500°F, melting asphalt.

19. Arthur 'Bomber' Harris.

20. The Avro Lancaster Bomber.

21. B) 2.7 million tonnes.

22. Nissen huts.

23. Lancaster, Stirling and Halifax bombers.

24. It was the first night raid to consist of 1,000 bombers.

25. C) Pathfinders.

26. Baedeker raids.

27. The dams of the Möhne and Sorpe rivers. They became known as the Dambuster raids.

28. The Norden bombsight.

29. The Regensburg–Schweinfurt raids.

30. C) Window.

31. The Flying Fortress.

32. Curtis LeMay.

33. B) Clark Gable.

34. An attack by US bombers on the Romanian oilfields at Ploesti.

35. B) Christmas trees.

36. Fiction. It was known as the 'Zoo' flak tower.

37. Nazi leader Hermann Göring remarked that if the RAF ever bombed Berlin, he was to be called 'Meyer'.

38. 'Submarines'.

39. 'Night music' or *Schräge musik*. *Schräge musik* or 'slanting music' was a German term for jazz, and used here it referenced the slanting angle of the night fighter's guns.

40. Barnes Wallis.

41. President Roosevelt.

42. C) 50,000. This was a similar number to those from British and Commonwealth air crews.

43. Oflags were for captured officers, whilst Stalags were for enlisted men.

44. Colditz, Oflag IV-C.

45. B) Glider.

46. 'Home runs'.

47. A Red Cross food parcel.

48. B) He escaped from Canada.

49. Geneva Convention.

50. Tarawa.

51. C) Landing Vehicle Tracked.

52. Makin Atoll.

53. South West Pacific and the South and Central Pacific.

54. Rabaul.

55. A) The Battle of Bismarck Sea.

56. B) Skip bombing.

57. William Halsey.

58. Rabaul.

59. John F. Kennedy.

60. They decided to bypass heavily defended islands, using sea and air power to instead cut off those islands.

61. 'Seabees'.

62. Truth.

63. The Chance-Vought Corsair.

64. C) Japanese troops ended the battle in a mass suicidal charge.

65. Battle of Kursk.

66. To close the Soviet salient in their lines at Kursk.

67. Panther tank.

68. Sturmovik.

69. C) 5 July 1943.

70. Nebelwerfer.

71. The southern flank near Belgorod.

72. The Soviet Fifth Guards Tank Army and the German Fourth Panzer Army.

73. Prokhorovka.

74. C) Orel.

75. B) Eight.

76. B) *Stal* or 'Steel'.

77. The T-34 tanks got close to the heavier German panzers and 'swarmed' the German tanks.

78. B) One million.

79. Truth. But the Soviets replaced the losses, whilst the Germans could not.

80. Orel and Kharkov.

81. Michael Wittman.

82. Sicily.

83. Italy – it was his view that the Allies should advance through mainland Italy and into Central Europe.

84. Patton and Montgomery.

85. Truth. The number of troops, ships and planes was similar to the amount used in the invasion of France a year later.

86. This was a deception operation to mislead the Germans into thinking the Allies were planning to attack Sardinia or Greece, and that the attack on Sicily was merely a diversion.

87. Truth, the body was identified in the 1990s to be that of Glyndwr Michael.

88. B) *The Man Who Never Was*.

89. The US Seventh Army and British Eighth Army.

90. Syracuse.

91. B) 10 July 1943.

92. Landing Craft Infantry.

93. Fiction. The mafia greeted US soldiers as liberators.

94. The Hermann Göring Panzer Division.

95. B) The 'Big Red One'.

96. Pietro Badoglio.

97. C) Messina.

98. Truth. Eisenhower persuaded him to apologize to the troops and he escaped further sanctions.

99. Gran Sasso.

100. Otto Skorzeny.

101. B) 3 September 1943.

CHAPTER 8

Striking Back

1. At which two points did the British Eighth Army land in mainland Italy in 1943?

2. Name the location of US landings in Italy in September 1943? *On laser.*

3. Which general commanded the US Fifth Army during its landings in Italy?
   A) Mark Clark   B) George Patton   C) Dwight D. Eisenhower.

4. Which mountain chain, running up the centre of Italy, allowed the Germans to fortify a number of defensive lines?

5. The British favoured an extension of the Mediterranean campaign in mainland Italy although their US allies were less keen on the campaign. What reason did the British give for this strategy?

6. What name was given to the German defensive line that stretched along the River Garigliano in the west, across the Apennines, to the Adriatic coast?
   A) Siegfried Line   B) Cassino Line   C) Gustav Line.

7. In this photo, a bomber is flying over the Abruzzan Apennines. Name the aircraft.

8. The German defenders of which stronghold, that controlled access to the Liri Valley and Highway 6 to Rome, repelled repeated Allied attempts to capture it? *So mates in con.*

9. Where is location B, which saw an Allied amphibious landing that attempted to outflank the fortified Gustav Line?

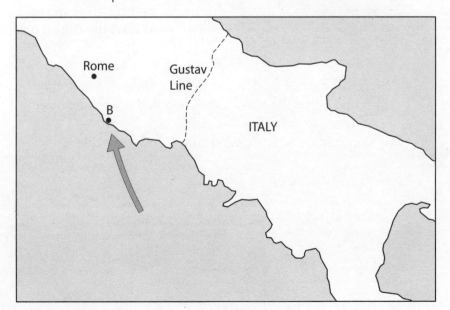

10. Truth or fiction? During the Allied advance along the Italian peninsula, the US Army was on the right side of Italy while the British advanced on the left side.

11. Between which two northern Italian towns did the Allies think the Germans would make their retreat, once Italy signed an armistice?

12. Operation Axis was a German operation to seize which major Italian city in 1943?

13. Following the surrender of Italy to the Allies in September 1943, how many Italian troops were seized as prisoners of war by the Germans?   A) 250,000   B) 400,000   C) 650,000.

14. Two German troopers are pictured fighting in Italy in 1944. Based on the type of helmets they are wearing, what type of troops are they?

15. What is the name of this hilltop stronghold in Italy, finally captured by the Allies in May 1944?

16. Operation Shingle was an Allied landing on 22 January 1944. Where was it?

17. Truth or fiction? The abbey at the centre of German defences on the Gustav Line was heavily bombed by the Allies. There were no German forces initially in the abbey, and they only fortified the ruins once the bombing had finished.

18. Where did Mussolini set up his puppet government of the Italian Social Republic, following his rescue by German special forces?

19. Which order of monks inhabited an abbey that was a crucial defensive position for the Germans in Italy in 1943–4? *Dice been nit.*

20. Who was German commander in chief in Italy from 1943?
    Trees braking sell.

21. Name the river near the Gustav Line which the Allies had to cross in their advance on Rome?
    A) Tiber B) Rapido C) Ponzi.

22. What did German scientists re-introduce to the Pontine Marshes, as revenge for the Italian surrender in 1943, which had an impact on both local civilians and Allied soldiers?

23. After landing in January 1944, in which month did Allied forces finally break out of the Anzio bridgehead?
    A) June B) May C) August.

24. Which German commanded troops that surrounded the Allies at Anzio in January 1944? *Hard seven broken a cenm.*

25. What nickname was given to a narrow salient that formed in the German lines following a British attack at Anzio in 1944?
    A) The Neck B) The Hand C) The Thumb.

26. Operation Diadem was a successful Allied operation in Italy in 1944. What was it?

27. The Germans used a number of new weapons during Allied landings at Anzio, including the Henschel Hs-293. What was this weapon?

28. In 1944, what location did French troops seize in the Gustav Line to the north-east of an important abbey stronghold?

29. At Anzio in February 1944, the Germans herded animals in front of their soldiers to clear minefields. Were the animals A) Goats B) Cows C) Sheep?

30. What was the name of the German remote-controlled detonation vehicle that was used at Anzio?

31. What nationality were the troops who captured the Italian abbey stronghold in May 1944, after months of heavy fighting?   A) American   B) New Zealander   C) Polish.

32. Truth or fiction? German forces constructed a new defensive line south of Rome in 1944 following the Allied landings at Anzio, called the Caesar Line since it followed the course of the Rubicon river.

33. An M7 105mm self-propelled gun comes ashore from a landing craft at Anzio, January 1944. What was its nickname due to the pulpit-like machine gun turret?

34. Operations Turtle and Buffalo were Allied plans to advance on which city in 1944?

35. What name was given to the German defensive line in northern Italy where German forces retreated in June 1944?

36. Why were the landings at Anzio in 1944 ultimately deemed to be a failure?

37. Name the British general in overall command of Allied Forces in Italy? *Hola lender draxa.*

38. Which Japanese base, located in the Caroline Islands, was attacked by US aircraft from mid-February 1944?
A) Rabaul   B) Tinian   C) Truk.

39. Which island group in the central Pacific consisted of four main islands: Saipan, Tinian, Rota and Guam?
A) The Philippines   B) The Carolines   C) The Marianas.

40. What was the Battle of the Philippine Sea in June 1944 nicknamed? Clue: this bird is a seasonal favourite.

41. Which US admiral was commander in chief of the US Pacific Fleet from 1941 to 1945? *Size n them crit.*

42. An American engineering battalion had the motto 'We build. We fight.' What was the battalion?

43. Which Pacific island was attacked by US forces on June 15 1944? *Pa as in.*

44. Which US torpedo bomber entered service in 1942, and counted future president George Bush as one of its pilots?

45. What was the impact for Japan of the loss of the Marianas island chain in 1944?
A) Japanese forces were no longer able to launch an invasion of Australia
B) US forces were now able to invade the Philippines
C) US bombers based in the Marianas were able to bomb the Japanese mainland.

46. In April 1944, Japanese forces launched a major attack in China with 600,000 troops. What were the two aims of this attack?

47. In February 1944, Japanese forces attacked through central Burma with the intention of invading which country?
A) China   B) India   C) Cambodia.

48. What was the name of Japan's 1944 attack through Burma, the last Japanese offensive of the war?   A) Operation U-Go
B) Operation U-For   C) Operation Go-For.

49. Which city in north-east India was attacked by Japanese troops in March 1944? *Ham lip.*

50. Which other town in north-east India, a particularly hilly location, was attacked by Japanese forces in 1944? *Oh a kim.*

51. Caved-in bunkers, seen here on Ito Hill (as the Japanese called it) in India, were captured following fierce fighting in 1944. By what English nickname was this hill known?

52. What was the nickname of the US long-range penetration jungle warfare unit? *Same malls rur rider.*

53. Truth or fiction? When Japanese troops attacked the Allied garrison in the most northerly besieged town in India, they would first shout, 'Give up!'

54. The siege of which Russian city was lifted on 27 January 1944? A) Moscow   B) Stalingrad   C) Leningrad.

55. On 30 March 1944, which two commanders were sacked as heads of German Army Group South and Centre in Russia?

56. On 19 March 1944, which former ally of Germany was occupied by German troops because Hitler feared that the country had made peace overtures to the Allies?
A) Romania   B) Hungary   C) Finland.

57. Which port on the Black Sea was captured by the Red Army on 10 April 1944? *Sad ose.*

58. In April 1943, although there was not yet a supreme commander, British General Frederick Morgan was appointed COSSAC. What did this stand for and what task was he given?

59. How many US troops were stationed in Britain by the end of 1943? A) 250,000   B) 560,000   C) 790,000.

60. Truth or fiction? When the initial plan for the invasion of Europe was finalized in July 1943, the area selected was the Pas de Calais, due to its proximity to the English coast.

61. What name was given to the wide-ranging German coastal defences situated along the coast of Europe, started in 1940?
A) Channel Wall   B) Atlantic Wall   C) European Sea Wall.

62. Which German building company was responsible for the many defences around the coast of occupied Europe? *Tintin goads a root.*

63. The Sherman Crab Mark II flail tank seen here was developed for the Allied invasion of Europe. What type of weapon was it intended to eliminate?

64. The 'Crab' and 'Crocodile' were just two types of specialist armoured vehicles developed by the Allies for the invasion of Europe. What was the nickname of this group of tanks and who were they named after?

65. What did the D in D-Day stand for?
A) Disembark   B) Day   C) Dog.

66. Which house, situated near Portsmouth in England, became the headquarters for Allied command in the run up to D-Day? *Who is stuck ohue.*

67. 'Our landings in the Cherbourg–Havre area have failed to gain a satisfactory foothold and I have withdrawn the troops. My decision to attack at this time and place was based upon the best information available. The troops, the air and the navy did all that bravery and devotion to duty could do. If any blame or fault attaches to the attempt it is mine alone.' This was written by General Eisenhower in June 1944, but why did he write it?

68. What name was given to the standard German anti-tank mine used extensively in Normandy? Clue: it is also the German word for 'plate' due to its appearance.

69. In an 'order of the day' message sent to all troops prior to D-Day, what two-word phrase did Eisenhower give to the upcoming invasion?
A) Great Invasion   B) Great Adventure   C) Great Crusade.

70. What operational codename was given to the Allied invasion of France in 1944?

71. Truth or fiction? The original plan for D-Day was to land forces on just two beaches.

72. What did German Field Marshals Rommel and von Rundstedt disagree on prior to D-Day?

73. What was the meaning of AMGOT, which was due to be implemented following the invasion of France?

74. What was Plan Fortitude?

75. Dummy landing craft, pictured, were used as decoys in harbours before D-Day. Which US general was the head of a fictitious First Army Group based in south-east England?

76. The Fourth British Army, a 'ghost' army stationed in northern Britain, was used to convince the Germans that the Allies were also planning to invade which occupied country? A) Netherlands   B) Denmark   C) Norway.

77. Which double agent, codenamed 'Garbo', was part of the D-Day deception and fed German intelligence information that the main Allied attack would be in the Pas de Calais?

78. How many beaches were finally selected for landings on D-Day?

79. Operation PLUTO was used to supply the invasion forces with fuel. What did PLUTO mean?

80. Truth or fiction? The invasion of occupied France was scheduled for 5 June 1944 but was put back one day due to bad weather.

81. Operation Ironside was an Allied D-Day deception. What was the plan?

82. Prior to the invasion, what did the planners of D-Day target with bombers?

83. Which beach in southern England saw the deaths of 749 US servicemen during a D-Day training exercise? *Tods san plans.*

84. What was the name of the three-man teams that were sent to France to align resistance groups to Allied aims prior to D-Day? A) SOE   B) Jedburgh   C) Delta.

85. British mathematician Arthur Thomas Doodson developed which item which greatly helped the planners of D-Day? A) A tide-prediction machine   B) Swimming tanks C) Rocket ships.

86. What nickname was given to German defensive posts fixed vertically into the ground to prevent gliders from landing in open areas?

87. Why was Exercise Tiger a disastrous rehearsal for D-Day?

88. Phoenix caissons, pictured, were an important component of which Allied innovation on D-Day?

89. What did the inflatable element of Duplex DD tanks enable the tanks to do? A) Fly B) Swim C) Bounce.

90. Who was the British group captain responsible for a crucial weather forecast prior to D-Day? *Gags set jam.*

91. Due to poor weather in the English Channel, what decision did German General Rommel take on 5 June 1944?

92. What type of adapted tank, pictured, was used on D-Day?

93. In order to disrupt German radar, what did Allied planes drop on the night of 5 June 1944 along the coast of France? A) Window B) Flares C) Pigeons.

94. Which two US airborne divisions dropped on the Cotentin peninsular in France during the night of D-Day?

95. What is the only surviving ship, along with USS *Laffey* and USS *Texas*, which took part in the naval bombardment on D-Day, and is now moored on the banks of the River Thames in London? *Them as flbs.*

96. What was Bénouville Bridge re-named following the successful British glider operation to capture it in the early hours of D-Day?
A) Caen Bridge B) Howard Bridge C) Pegasus Bridge.

97. What was the main objective of the Allied airborne operations in the early hours of D-Day?

98. Name this type of glider which was used to transport troops and supplies to Normandy?

99. On 6 June 1944, 132,000 ground troops were landed on the beaches of Normandy. What was the codename for the naval operation?

100. Truth or fiction? To confuse the Germans on D-Day, Allied planes dropped dummy parachutists that exploded on landing.

101. Which occupied Channel port was attacked by Free French forces on D-Day? *Hire u moats.*

ANSWERS

1. Reggio and Taranto.

2. Salerno.

3. A) Mark Clark.

4. The Apennines.

5. The Germans would tie up resources which they could otherwise use on the Eastern Front or against an invasion in France.

6. C) Gustav Line.

7. Martin Baltimore Mark IV bomber.

8. Monte Cassino.

9. Anzio.

10. Fiction. The US army was on the left and British armies were on the right flank.

11. Pisa and Rimini.

12. Rome.

13. C) 650,000.

14. German paratroopers.

15. Monte Cassino abbey.

16. Anzio.

17. Truth. Italian civilians were killed during the bombing raid and German forces occupied the ruins afterwards.

18. Salò on Lake Garda.

19. Benedictine.

20. Albert Kesselring.

21. B) Rapido.

22. They flooded much of the area and introduced malaria-carrying mosquitoes.

23. B) May.

24. Eberhard von Mackensen.

25. C) The Thumb.

26. A breakthrough on the Gustav Line at Cassino.

27. This was an anti-ship guided missile, or 'glide-bomb', with a rocket positioned underneath. It sunk and damaged a number of ships off Anzio.

28. Monte Belvedere.

29. C) Sheep.

30. Borgward IV heavy explosive carrier.

31. C) Polish.

32. Fiction. Although there was a Caesar Line, it was not named after the Rubicon, which is in north-east Italy.

33. The 'Priest'.

34. Rome.

35. The Gothic Line.

36. Despite tying down large numbers of Germans, the Anzio landings did not break the deadlock in Italy.

37. Harold Alexander.

38. C) Truk.

39. C) The Marianas.

40. 'The Great Marianas Turkey Shoot'.

41. Chester Nimitz.

42. US Navy Construction Battalions or 'Seabees'.

43. Saipan.

44. Grumman 'Avenger'

45. C) US bombers based in the Marianas were able to bomb the Japanese mainland.

46. To capture Allied airfields in China and to open up a land route for supplies from Indochina to Korea.

47. B) India.

48. A) Operation U-Go.

49. Imphal.

50. Kohima.

51. 'Scraggy Hill'.

52. 'Merrill's Marauders'.

53. Truth. This actually helped the defenders know they were coming.

54. C) Leningrad.

55. Erich von Manstein and Ewald von Kleist.

56. B) Hungary.

57. Odessa.

58. Chief of Staff to the Supreme Allied Commander. He was charged with making plans for the invasion of occupied France.

59. C) 790,000.

60. Fiction. The coast near Caen in Normandy was selected, but the Allies needed to deceive the Germans into thinking that the Pas de Calais would be the main invasion area.

61. B) Atlantic Wall.

62. Todt Organisation.

63. Mines. The beating of the ground by the 'flails' triggered the mines to explode.

64. 'Hobart's Funnies' named after British Major General Percy Hobart, who led the team that developed them.

65. B) Day.

66. Southwick House.

67. This was Eisenhower's 'failure letter', to be used in the event of a failed Allied landing.

68. The Tellermine.

69. C) 'Great Crusade'.

70. Operation Overlord.

71. Fiction. The original plan was for landings on three beaches.

72. Rommel wanted the panzers to be close to the invasion beaches, fearing they would be hit by Allied planes whilst trying to deploy. Von Rundstedt wanted to hold them back to use when the landing location was fully known.

73. Allied Military Government for Occupied Territories. It was not implemented in France due to a new government being formed quickly following liberation.

74. A series of deception plans designed to keep the Germans guessing where the Allied landings in France would take place.

75. General George Patton.

76. C) Norway.

77. Juan Pujol García. German troops were stationed in the Pas de Calais for two months after the invasion.

78. Five beaches.

79. It stands for 'Pipeline Underwater Transport of Oil', although it has often been misquoted as standing for 'Pipeline Under the Ocean'.

80. Truth. The invasion was originally scheduled for 5 June 1944.

81. To deceive the Germans into believing that there would be an Allied landing in the Bay of Biscay.

82. Key infrastructure leading to the Normandy area was targeted, effectively 'sealing' the combat zone.

83. Slapton Sands.

84. B) Jedburgh.

85. A) A tide-prediction machine.

86. 'Rommel's asparagus'.

87. German E-boats attacked the exercise in the English Channel, leading to US losses. It was kept secret during the war.

88. They were part of the artificial Mulberry harbours.

89. B) Swim. A number sank on D-Day due to the tanks being launched too far from shore.

90. James Stagg.

91. He left Normandy for a trip back to Germany to celebrate his wife's birthday.

92. Sherman DD (Duplex Drive) amphibious tank, with its inflatable skirt lowered.

93. A) Metal strips known as 'Window'.

94. 82nd and 101st US Airborne Divisions.

95. HMS *Belfast*, now a branch of Imperial War Museums.

96. C) Pegasus Bridge.

97. To secure the flanks of the Allied invasion beaches.

98. Horsa glider, seen here at a landing zone in June 1944.

99. Operation Neptune.

100. Truth. The dummies were given the names 'Rupert' by the British and 'Oscar' by the Americans.

101. Ouistreham.

CHAPTER 9

Two Fronts

1. Truth or fiction? The Allied landings on D-Day were feared compromised before they started, as a number of codewords appeared as answers to crossword puzzles in newspapers prior to the landings taking place.

2. Name the beaches of the Normandy landings at A, C and E.

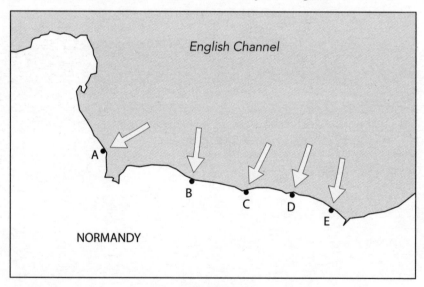

3. Which fortified clifftop position at Omaha Beach was attacked by a ranger battalion? *The coin pudo.*

4. What nationality were the troops that landed at Omaha Beach on D-Day? A) British B) Canadian C) American.

5. What error occurred on Utah Beach when the US 4th Division landed on D-Day?

6. On which village in Normandy were US paratroopers mistakenly dropped, leading to heavy casualties amongst the paratroopers? *Meets elisè regain.*

7. Name the beach, pictured, where troops are coming ashore from landing craft on D-Day.

8. Truth or fiction? US paratrooper John Steele was caught on a church spire when parachuting over Normandy and played dead while German troops shot at him and his comrades.

9. Bad weather and strong German defences delayed the British assault at Sword Beach. As a result, which key location was not taken on the first day?

10. Which Normandy town was the objective for British troops landing at Gold Beach on D-Day? Clue: this is a famous tapestry.

11. US troops suffered such heavy casualties at Omaha Beach that which word has now become associated with the landing there?   A) Deathly   B) Deadly   C) Bloody.

12. In this photo, a survivor from a sunken landing craft is being helped ashore at Omaha Beach. Which US commander considered abandoning the assault there?

13. Which airfield near Caen was not captured during the early stages of D-Day, hampering Allied efforts to establish air bases within the invasion area?

14. How many casualties did the Allies suffer during the D-Day landings?   A) 5,000   B) 9,000   C) 19,000.

15. Which female journalist went ashore on D-Day having sneaked on to a hospital ship and hidden in a toilet? *The mall or hagrn.*

16. What was 'Duke of Normandy', the first to bring back news on D-Day of British airborne landings?   A) A fishing boat   B) A carrier pigeon   C) A Wellington bomber.

17. Which war artist produced drawings of D-Day after crossing the Channel one week after the landings? *Doze zen ward dira.*

18. Journalists reporting on the D-Day landings were part of the British AFPU. What did AFPU stand for?
    A) Allied Films Purchasing Unit
    B) Army Film and Photographic Unit
    C) Allied Film Patrons Unit.

19. Where did British and US forces meet on 7 June 1944, having advanced from Gold and Omaha Beaches? *Spent or biens.*

20. Truth or fiction? The Germans were unable to launch immediate panzer counterattacks against the Normandy beaches because Hitler would have had to give the order, but he was asleep and no-one was prepared to wake him up.

21. What nickname, the German for 'hunter bomber', did German troops give Allied fighter-bombers in Normandy?

22. What is the name for the Normandy countryside with high, dense hedgerows, small fields and sunken lanes, and how did German troops use this to their advantage?

23. What was Operation Perch, which took place between 7 and 14 June?

24. What did US troops encounter on the Cotentin peninsular following D-Day?
A) A range of hills   B) Waterlogged and flooded land
C) Sandy soil and tanks sinking.

25. Name the rocket-firing British fighter-bomber, pictured, which along with P-47 Thunderbolts, was a formidable weapon during the battle of Normandy?

26. Which French town was captured by US airborne troops following the D-Day landings? *Race nant.*

27. What was the nickname of US Major General Lawton Collins, whose forces cut off the Cotentin peninsula?

28. Which French port was captured by the Allies on 27 June 1944?   A) Dieppe   B) Boulogne   C) Cherbourg.

29. The British operations Epsom and Charnwood were designed to outflank and capture which French city?

30. Where did German Tiger tanks inflict a devastating ambush on British tanks in Normandy? *Level or is bacg.*

31. Operation Goodwood was launched by British forces on 18 July 1944. What advantage did this gain the Allies?

32. Where did US forces clash with German armour during a major German counterattack, ordered by Hitler, to try to contain an Allied breakout from Normandy?

33. What did Operations Epsom and Charnwood convince German commanders that they could no longer do?

34. Truth or fiction? Günther von Kluge took over from Erwin Rommel during the Battle of Normandy due to Rommel contracting food poisoning.

35. Which crucial road junction situated at the base of the Cotentin peninsula was captured by US forces? *Raves anch.*

36. What was the Allied Operation Totalize in Normandy?

37. Who took command of the US Third Army and led the Allied breakout in Normandy?

38. In this photograph, masses of wrecked German vehicles litter a road. What name was given to the 'pocket' created by the link-up of US and British troops in Normandy?

39. How many German troops were encircled in Normandy when the Allies linked up at Chambois on 19 August 1944? A) 10,000 B) 30,000 C) 50,000.

40. What was the result of Allied success in the Battle of Normandy in 1944?

41. What happened to the U-boat bases on the French Atlantic coast following the Allied breakout from Normandy?

42. Which event happened at the 'Wolf's Lair', Hitler's headquarters, on 20 July 1944?

43. Which colonel became chief of staff for the German Replacement Army on 1 July 1944? *Begun fasten sovar fulc.*

44. What was Operation Valkyrie?

45. Which two German field marshals committed suicide following the failed attempt to assassinate Hitler?

46. What name was given to a major Soviet offensive launched on 23 June 1944?

47. In which country did the main Soviet offensive take place in the summer of 1944?

48. Which city was liberated on 3 July 1944 by advancing Red Army troops? A) Smolensk B) Opochka C) Minsk.

49. Who replaced Ernst Busch as commander of German Army Group Centre in 1944?

50. Which river, marking the pre-war border between Poland and Russia, was reached on 20 July 1944 by Soviet forces? A) Dnieper B) Bug C) Prut.

51. The outskirts of which city were reached by Soviet troops on 14 September 1944? Clue: the local population would start an uprising.

52. Who was the Polish commander of the Home Army in the summer of 1944? *Stood bare kózow u smirk*

53. What began at 'W-hour'– 5 p.m. on 1 August 1944?

54. Truth or fiction? With Soviet forces just outside Warsaw, Stalin dropped weapons to Polish insurgents without parachutes, making the weapons which landed un-workable.

55. Which French city saw an uprising begin on 19 August 1944? A) Rouen B) Paris C) Chartres

56. Who was the commander of Free French forces in France and liberated Paris? *Hi cell piper clep.*

57. The resistance movement in Paris in August 1944 was known as the FFI. What did FFI mean?
A) Free French Interior   B) French Free Interior
C) French Forces of the Interior.

58. Who was the German military governor of Paris, ordered by Hitler to destroy the city on 23 August 1944? *Zoo chin lvtt.*

59. French civilians run for cover as a German sniper opens fire from buildings in Paris on 26 August 1944. When did the Germans surrender in Paris?

60. What was the convoy system known as the 'Red Ball Express'?
A) Trucks delivering fuel to the front from Normandy
B) Flights from England bringing mail
C) Allied troops behind enemy lines escaping.

61. What did the secret weapons, called *Vergeltungswaffen* by the Germans, become known as?
A) R-weapons   B) V-weapons   C) RV-weapons.

62. What first landed at Clapham, in south London, on 13 June 1944?

63. Which German developed the Nazi rocket programme and went on to work in the US on the moon rockets?
A) Braun von Werner   B) Wernher von Braun
C) Wraun von Berner.

64. What nickname was given to German flying bombs that were powered by a jet engine and launched from ramps? *Dog solubed.*

65. In which area of London did the first V-2 weapon fall in September 1944?
A) Hammersmith   B) Chiswick   C) Ealing.

66. This photo shows a German V-2 rocket being launched. Which two Belgian cities suffered attacks from V-2 weapons?

67. How fast did a German V-2 rocket descend to earth whilst carrying its warhead?
A) 2,410 kph (1,500 mph)   B) 3,200 kph (2,000 mph)
C) 4,000 kph (2,500 mph).

68. Which two islands became the main focus for US attempts to regain the Philippines in 1944?

69. On 25 October 1944, the US escort carrier, *St Lô*, was attacked and sunk by what in the Philippines? Clue: there was no coming back from this.

70. Which battle was the last fleet-versus-fleet action between Japan and the US in 1944?

71. Which German defensive line was reached by US troops in September 1944? *Freed in seigil.*

72. Operation Market Garden was a daring Allied operation to do what in 1944?

73. If the airborne element of Operation Market Garden was codenamed 'Market', what did 'Garden' refer to in the plan? Clue: there is a link here.

74. What does the word *kamikaze*, applied to the Japanese suicide attacks, actually mean?
A) Total war   B) Honor with death   C) Divine wind.

75. Cromwell tanks of the Welsh Guards cross the bridge at Nijmegen during Operation Market Garden. Which bridge proved too far for Allied ground forces?

76. What information was disregarded by planners of Operation Market Garden, resulting in disastrous consequences for Allied airborne troops?

77. How many airborne troops were deployed by the Allies on the first day of Operation Market Garden?
A) 10,000   B) 20,000   C) 5,000.

78. What two reasons explained the slow progress of British XXX Corps during its attempt to link airborne landings in Operation Market Garden?

79. Truth or fiction? British airborne forces were blighted by poor radio sets at Arnhem, which hindered communication with incoming aircraft.

80. Name the location of British airborne headquarters near Arnhem during Operation Market Garden? *Boost e reek.*

81. Who led XXX Corps during Operation Market Garden in its attempt to link up with US and British airborne troops?

82. Which key resource in Romania was seized by Soviet forces on 2 September 1944? Clue: black gold.

83. On 18 October 1944, Himmler announced that which organization would be formed in Germany?

84. Which German city was the first to fall to US troops following heavy fighting in October 1944?
A) Frankfurt B) Cologne C) Aachen.

85. Which densely wooded area in Germany saw heavy US infantry losses during fierce fighting in November 1944?

86. What was nicknamed 'repple depple'?
A) Repeated demands   B) Replacement depot
C) Replenish daily.

87. Which Belgian town (A) became surrounded by German forces in December 1944?

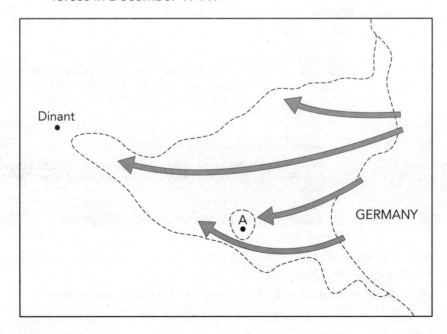

88. Codenamed 'Watch on the Rhine', what was a German plan in October 1944?

89. Who was the commander of the German Sixth Panzer Army during the winter offensive in 1944?

90. Which US major general commanded VIII Corps in the Ardennes in December 1944? *Dont my or tidel.*

91. This photo shows troops from the First SS Panzer Division in December 1944. What type of vehicle are they driving?

92. On what date did German forces launch a surprise attack through the Ardennes in 1944?
A) 9 December   B) 16 December   C) 20 December.

93. Truth or fiction? Germans dressed in US uniforms infiltrated behind Allied lines, and were part of a plot to assassinate General Eisenhower.

94. Which German commander of the First SS Panzer Division was known for his ruthless approach during the Ardennes battle?

95. Where were captured US troops massacred by advancing SS forces in the Ardennes? *Dame mly.*

96. Which geographical feature remained in US hands from the start of the German winter offensive in the Ardennes?
A) Elsenborn Ridge
B) Houffliaze Ridge
C) Malmedy Ridge.

97. In the photo opposite, Sergeant John Opanowski emerges from a dug-out as US troops are pinned down by crack panzer divisions. Which town proved to be the centre of stubborn US resistance in the Ardennes?

98. What was the key factor that enabled initial German success in the Ardennes offensive in December 1944?

99. Operation *Bodenplatte* or 'Baseplate' took place on 1 January 1945. What was it?

100. An American ambulance passes an abandoned German tank in December 1944. What type of tank is it?

101. What reply did the US commander give to the Germans outside Bastogne in response to an ultimatum for US troops to surrender?
A) 'Go to hell'   B) 'Nuts'   C) 'Adios'.

102. What name was given to the winter offensive in the Ardennes, due to the shape the German advance left in the Allied lines?

ANSWERS

1. Truth. The crossword compilers were arrested, but released after investigations showed that it was a coincidence.

2. Utah (A), Gold (C) and Sword (E).

3. Pointe du Hoc.

4. C) American.

5. The current caused landing craft to veer away from the correct beach, landing 1,800 m (2,000 yards) south of the intended site. The area was only lightly defended so US troops soon moved inland.

6. Sainte-Mère-Eglise.

7. Juno Beach.

8. Truth. The incident happened at Sainte-Mère-Eglise.

9. The town of Caen.

10. Bayeux.

11. C) 'Bloody' Omaha.

12. General Bradley. Before the decision was made, news came back that troops were advancing and the landings continued.

13. Carpiquet airfield.

14. B) 9,000, with the most casualties sustained at one beach – Omaha.

15. Martha Gellhorn.

16. B) Carrier pigeon.

17. Edward Ardizzone.

18. B) Army Film and Photographic Unit.

19. Port-en-Bessin.

20. Truth. It wasn't until the afternoon of 6 June that Hitler gave approval.

21. '*Jabos*', short for Jäger bombers.

22. The bocage, where ambush by German forces carrying hand-held rocket launchers had an impact on Allied tanks.

23. A British operation to outflank Caen to the west of the town.

24. B) Waterlogged and flooded land.

25. Hawker Typhoon.

26. Carentan.

27. 'Lightning Joe'.

28. C) Cherbourg.

29. Caen.

30. Villers-Bocage.

31. It kept the bulk of German forces in the eastern British sector, which helped US troops to break out with Operation Cobra.

32. Mortain.

33. The Germans believed there was no longer any prospect of driving the Allies back to the sea.

34. Fiction. Von Kluge did take over Rommel's command, but this was because Rommel was injured by Allied aircraft on 17 July 1944.

35. Avranches.

36. This was a Canadian advance south of Caen.

37. General George Patton.

38. The Falaise Pocket.

39. C) 50,000.

40. It opened up a second front in Europe, and the Germans lost a large amount of men and equipment.

41. Hitler declared that no port should be given up, so they were placed under siege by the Allies.

42. A bomb exploded in an attempt to assassinate Adolf Hitler.

43. Claus von Stauffenberg.

44. This was originally a German plan for the emergency continuity of government. It was adapted by anti-Hitler conspirators for the aftermath of their proposed assassination of Hitler in July 1944.

45. Field Marshals Rommel and von Kluge.

46. Operation Bagration.

47. Byelorussia, present-day Belarus.

48. C) Minsk.

49. Walter Model.

50. B) River Bug.

51. Warsaw.

52. Tadeusz Bór-Komorowski.

53. The Warsaw Uprising.

54. Truth. Stalin favoured installing a puppet government which would be friendly to Moscow, so had no real desire to help the Poles in the Warsaw Uprising.

55. B) Paris.

56. Philippe Leclerc.

57. C) French Forces of the Interior.

58. Von Choltitz.

59. 25 August 1944, but some snipers were still active the next day.

60. A) Trucks delivering fuel to the front from Normandy.

61. B) V-weapons. *Vergeltungswaffen* translates as 'revenge weapons'.

62. The V-1 flying bomb.

63. B) Wernher von Braun.

64. Doodlebugs.

65. B) Chiswick.

66. Brussels and Antwerp.

67. C) 4,000 kph (2,500 mph).

68. Leyte and Luzon.

69. A kamikaze suicide attack.

70. The Battle of Leyte Gulf.

71. Siegfried Line.

72. Seize Dutch bridges and advance over the Rhine.

73. It referred to land-based forces who would link up with the separate airborne landings.

74. C) 'Divine wind'.

75. The bridge at Arnhem.

76. Dutch resistance reported the presence of two SS panzer divisions in the area around Arnhem.

77. B) 20,000.

78. They suffered heavy German counterattacks along a narrow corridor of advance. The bridge at Wilhelmine Canal near Eindhoven was also destroyed, leading to a delay of 36 hours.

79. Truth. Many re-supply drops fell into German hands.

80. Oosterbeek.

81. General Sir Brian Horrocks.

82. The Ploesti oilfields.

83. The *Volkssturm*, a local defence militia.

84. C) Aachen.

85. The Hürtgen Forest.

86. B) Replacement depot.

87. Bastogne.

88. This was a German counterattack through the Ardennes, in an attempt to divide the Allied armies in two.

89. Sepp Dietrich.

90. Troy Middleton.

91. A *Schwimmwagen*, an amphibious 'swimming' car.

92. B) 16 December.

93. Fiction. German troops did infiltrate, and Allied intelligence thought Eisenhower was the target based on false reports from captured Germans.

94. Joachim Peiper.

95. Malmedy.

96. A) Elsenborn Ridge.

97. Bastogne.

98. Poor winter weather grounded Allied aircraft.

99. A German air operation to destroy Allied aircraft on the ground. The operation was a disaster for the Germans with many experienced pilots lost.

100. A German Tiger II tank. Also known as a 'King Tiger'.

101. B) 'Nuts'. It was General Anthony McAuliffe's initial verbal response to the ultimatum.

102. The Battle of the Bulge.

CHAPTER 10

Endgame and Aftermath

1. What was Operation *Nordwind* or North Wind, the last German offensive in the west during World War II?

2. Truth or fiction? The Netherlands would remain under German occupation north of the River Maas until the end of the war, and the Germans stopped the import of food as reprisal for helping the Allies.

3. 'Grand Slam' bombs were dropped on Germany aimed at bridges and viaducts, and, even when they did not strike directly, still caused damage. Why was this?
   A) The bomb produced an earthquake effect
   B) The bomb split into many little bombs
   C) The bomb was released at low altitude.

4. What type of weapon was the V-3?
   A) A rocket-powered tank
   B) An airship filled with napalm   C) A long-range gun.

5. Name Hitler's chalet, which was part of his mountain-top estate the Berghof? *Least genes.*

6. In the photo opposite is the mountain complex containing Adolf Hitler's chalet at Obersalzburg. Which Bavarian town did this complex overlook?

7. Which German city was attacked on 13–14 February 1945 by Allied bombers, leading to a firestorm?

8. Name this German jet, which first saw service in 1944.

9. Which passenger ship was torpedoed in the Baltic Sea on 30 January 1945 while evacuating German troops and civilians from the Baltic port of Gotenhafen (Gdynia)?

10. Which Axis capital fell to Soviet forces on 13 February 1945 following fierce fighting, which led to reprisals on civilians?

11. How many refugees are estimated to have been fleeing through Germany ahead of the Soviets in February 1945?
A) 3 million
B) 8 million
C) 12 million.

12. Which city in Poland, designated 'fortress', held out for a month against Soviet forces? *Oz nnap*

13. Which complex in Poland was liberated by Soviet forces on 27 January 1945?

14. What was the escarpment, overlooking the Oder River, which would become the last line of defence of Berlin from the east?   A) Oder Heights   B) Berlin Heights   C) Seelow Heights.

15. Which Japanese commander on the Philippine island of Luzon finally surrendered with his troops on 2 September 1945? *Green as lay ma a hit.*

16. Which city in the Philippines saw fierce fighting in 1945, leading to the deaths of one in eight of its population?   A) Mindanao   B) Manila   C) Mindondo.

17. Which Japanese city was devastated by a US air raid on 9 March 1945?

18. Which bridge over the Rhine, south of Bonn, was captured intact by US troops on 7 March 1945? *Game ner.*

19. What was the objective of the Allied Operation Varsity?   A) To drop troops in Berlin   B) To drop troops on the east bank of the Rhine   C) To drop troops in Bastogne.

20. Pioneers lay a smoke screen on 23 March 1945, during preparations for crossing which river?

21. What name was given to the encirclement of a large number of German troops in April 1945?
A) The Courland Pocket
B) The Berlin Pocket
C) The Ruhr Pocket.

22. In early 1945, the Germans transferred prisoners of war, usually on foot, from Eastern Europe into Western Germany. What are these transfers known as?

23. Truth or fiction? SCAF-252 was an Allied signal sent to Stalin in March 1945, assuring him that the Allies would advance south of Berlin, leaving the German capital to the Soviets.

24. In April 1945, US and British troops discovered which two German concentration camps, hardening the Allies' response to the Nazi regime?
A) Auschwitz and Majdanek
B) Treblinka and Sobibor
C) Buchenwald and Bergen-Belsen.

25. Operation Manna was an Allied food supply operation in spring 1945. Where did it take place?

26. Crowds watch the destruction of the last hut at Belsen, after the camp was evacuated. When it was liberated, what disease was prevalent in Belsen due to the conditions in the camp?

27. What order was given by Hitler in March 1945 to destroy key infrastructure in Germany? *Done or rer.*

28. Where did US and Soviet troops meet on 25 April 1945? A) Berlin   B) Torgau   C) Potsdam.

29. Following the fall of Berlin on 2 May 1945, Soviet soldiers raise their flag in victory on top of which ruined building?

30. Under which building was the *Führerbunker* situated in Berlin?

31. On what date did the Soviet armies begin the final assault on Berlin in 1945?
A) 10 April
B) 16 April
C) 20 April.

32. On his birthday in 1945, prominent Nazis urged Hitler to leave Berlin for Bavaria. He didn't, but a great many Nazi leaders did flee before Berlin was surrounded. What has this mass departure become known as?

33. 21 April 1945 saw what final act by the western Allies in Berlin?

34. Which concentration camp was liberated by US troops on 28 April 1945, resulting in many of the camp guards being shot?

35. Truth or fiction? Hermann Göring, who escaped to Bavaria, suggested to Hitler that he, Göring, should take over leadership of the Reich. Instead, Hitler placed Göring under house arrest.

36. Who was the husband of Eva Braun's sister, shot as he attempted to flee Berlin? *Rhine game len fen.*

37. Truth or fiction? When Hitler married Eva Braun in the bunker on 28 April 1945, the witnesses were his dog Blondi and Joseph Goebbels.

38. Truth or fiction? Nazi Propaganda Minister Joseph Goebbels and his wife Magda killed all six of their children before committing suicide themselves outside Hitler's bunker in May 1945?

39. Bernard Montgomery receives a German delegation surrendering at his headquarters on 3 May 1945. Where was this?

40. On what day in 1945 did US President Roosevelt die? A) 12 April   B) 13 April   C) 14 April.

41. Who was US vice-president in April 1945? *Arty man ruhr.*

42. In which city were the bodies of Mussolini and his mistress put on public display following their execution on 28 April 1945?   A) Rome   B) Bologna   C) Milan.

43. In February 1945, why did US forces land on the volcanic island of Iwo Jima, which was held by a strong force of 23,000 Japanese troops?

44. In this photo, landing craft approach the island of Iwo Jima. What is the name of the mountain surrounded by smoke?

45. Which US Marine divisions took part in the landings on the first day at Iwo Jima?   A) 2nd and 3rd Divisions B) 3rd and 4th Divisions   C) 4th and 5th Divisions.

46. Which US escort carrier was sunk off Iwo Jima on 21 February 1945 by a kamikaze attack? *Makes bus as cris.*

47. Truth or fiction? The commander of Japanese forces on Iwo Jima refused permission for his troops to take part in suicidal '*banzai*' charges. He thought that the Japanese defensive positions on the island were so strong that the Americans would suffer far greater casualties by trying to assault them.

48. Nicknamed the 'Zippo', what type of modified Sherman tank was used by US marines to clear positions on Iwo Jima?

49. How many Medals of Honor, America's highest military decoration, were awarded to US troops on Iwo Jima? A) 5 B) 18 C) 27.

50. An aerial view of Iwo Jima, where photographer Joe Rosenthal asked the marines to re-enact the moment they planted the 'Stars and Stripes'. The photograph was later used as a model for a memorial. Where is this memorial?

51. From an estimated force of 23,000 troops on Iwo Jima, how many Japanese surrendered when the island was taken by US forces? A) Less than 2,000 B) Less than 1,000 C) Less than 300.

52. Which island, largest of the Ryuku group, was attacked by US forces on 1 April 1945? *Wink a oa.*

53. Operation Ten-Go was a Japanese kamikaze mission in April 1945 involving which Japanese battleship?

54. Truth or fiction? The Japanese weapon named *Ohka*, meaning 'Cherry Blossom', was a piloted bomb.

55. In this photo, an American marine dashes for cover on Okinawa. What was the name of the citadel from which Japanese commanders directed the defence of the island?

56. Which US general was killed on Okinawa on 18 June 1945, just four days before the island surrendered?

57. Truth or fiction? Due to the fanatical Japanese defence on Okinawa, losses on both sides were high, with most Japanese troops choosing suicide rather than surrendering.

58. How many suicide attacks were estimated to have taken place against US naval forces in 1945 off the island of Okinawa? A) 500 B) 995 C) 1,465.

59. Which strategic position, a rise of land approximately 548 metres (600 yards) southeast of Mashiki in Okinawa, was taken after heavy fighting by the 96th US Infantry Division? A) Shuri Ridge B) Cactus Ridge C) Porcupine Ridge.

60. What was Operation Starvation, a US plan which began in March 1945?

61. Which US Air Force chief was transferred to the Far East in 1944 and successfully switched US tactics from high-level bombing to low-level night attacks? *Limey a curts.*

62. A *Fu-Go* was the first ever inter-continental weapon. Over 9,000 were launched towards the end of the war. What were they?

63. What percentage of Tokyo's urban area is estimated to have been destroyed by fire by the war's end? A) 25 per cent B) 50 per cent C) 75 per cent.

64. Who replaced Winston Churchill at the Potsdam Conference following Churchill's defeat in the British General Election in July 1945?

65. What four 'Ds' were agreed by the Allies for Germany following the end of the European war?

66. What choice was given to Japan in the Potsdam Declaration on 2 August 1945?

67. On 21 July 1945, whilst at the Potsdam Conference, President Truman received a telegram confirming what news? A) Plans to invade Japan B) Confirmation that the Soviets had started an atomic weapon programme C) Confirmation of a US atomic bomb detonation in the New Mexico desert.

68. The words 'No white cross for Stevie' were written by Major John Moynihan on what device in 1945?

69. Which Japanese city was the target for the first US atomic bomb on 6 August 1945?
A) Osaka   B) Kyoto   C) Hiroshima.

70. What was the name of the US plane which dropped the first atomic bomb and who piloted it?

71. The US plane which dropped the first atomic bomb set off from which Pacific island air base?

72. In this photo, which prominent building in the foreground is still standing following the first ever atomic explosion, the ruins of which now serve as a peace memorial?

73. The 'mushroom cloud' over a second Japanese city, photographed from an escorting American B-29 plane. Which city was the target and when?

74. Which plane dropped the second atomic bomb and who piloted it?

75. Which radioactive material was used in the second US atomic bomb? Clue: this material could be partly a distant planet.

76. Which country invaded Manchuria on 9 August 1945 and went to war with Japan?

77. Truth or fiction? Following the dropping of the atomic bombs, some army officers in Japan attempted a coup to prevent the broadcast of a radio message by Emperor Hirohito calling for all Japanese forces to lay down their weapons.

78. Following the atomic explosions in 1945, how many people are estimated to have perished instantly in each city from the blasts?
    A) 100,000 and 50,000
    B) 25,000 and 35,000
    C) 70,000 and 50,000.

79. The formal surrender of Japan was not signed until 2 September 1945. Which US commander presided over the signing and where did it take place?

80. How high are modern estimates of the total death toll from World War II?
    A) 55 to 70 million
    B) 25 to 50 million
    C) 75 to 100 million.

81. With the end of the war in Europe, millions of people found themselves widely spread across the continent as DPs. What did DP mean?
    A) Deprived People
    B) Displaced Person
    C) Don't Protect.

82. Which Allied plan for Germany, named after a US secretary of state, called for all industry to be diminished and destroyed, but was later dropped after the war and never implemented?

83. What was Emperor Hirohito of Japan made to concede publicly in 1946?
    A) That he was responsible for the war
    B) That he was not divine
    C) That he wanted to step down as emperor.

84. Name the city where Nazi leaders stood trial for war crimes from November 1945? *Merge burn.*

85. Following his conviction for war crimes, which senior Nazi leader committed suicide in 1945 prior to his execution?
    A) Heinrich Himmler
    B) Martin Bormann
    C) Hermann Göring.

86. In 1948, who became the only head of government to be executed for war crimes during World War II?

87. Which Nazi war criminal was captured in 1960 in Argentina, and was tried and executed in Israel? *Fame chain nold.*

88. Which organization, widely dismissed by historians as never having existed, is supposed to have helped Nazis escape from Europe to South America?

89. Winston Churchill said in a speech in March 1946, 'From Stettin in the Baltic to Trieste in the Adriatic, an iron curtain has descended across the continent.' Where did he make this speech? (Reproduced with the permission of Curtis Brown, London, on behalf of the Estate of Winston S. Churchill, ©The Estate of Winston S. Churchill)

90. Which organization had its first meeting in London on 10
January 1946?
A) NATO Alliance
B) UN General Assembly
C) International Monetary Fund.

91. What began on 23 November 1946 in Southeast Asia?

92. What US aid programme was announced in June 1946 with
the aim of rebuilding shattered post-war economies?
A) The Truman Plan
B) The Marshall Plan
C) The Winston Plan.

93. Which former British possession was granted independence
on 15 August 1947 and was subsequently partitioned?
Clue: this sub-continent has a large population.

94. Which Middle East state was proclaimed on 14 May 1948?

95. Codenamed Operation 'Plain Fare' by the British and
'Vittles' by the Americans, what was this post-war operation
in 1948?

96. Which state was proclaimed on 1 October 1949, following
the end of many years of civil war?

97. Which two blocs formed in the Cold War in 1949 and 1955, with the East–West German border as the dividing line?

98. What happened on 29 August 1949 in Kazakhstan?

99. In the photo opposite, a Douglas C-54 Skymaster is watched by a crowd of German civilians. In what year was the Soviet blockade of Berlin lifted?

100. Which former concentration camp has the words 'Never Again', carved in multiple languages on a grey wall, in memory of the war?
A) Auschwitz
B) Bergen-Belsen
C) Dachau.

ANSWERS

1. A German attack on US forces in Alsace.

2. Truth. There was a famine in the Netherlands during the winter of 1944–5.

3. A) The bomb produced an earthquake effect.

4. C) A long-range gun.

5. Eagle's Nest.

6. Berchtesgaden.

7. Dresden.

8. Messerschmitt Me 262.

9. The *Wilhelm Gustloff*, leading to the loss of at least 5,300 lives.

10. Budapest.

11. B) 8 million.

12. Poznan.

13. Auschwitz.

14. C) Seelow Heights.

15. General Yamashita.

16. B) Manila.

17. Tokyo.

18. Remagen.

19. B) To drop troops on the east bank of the Rhine.

20. The Rhine.

21. C) The Ruhr Pocket.

22. Death marches.

23. Truth. Eisenhower assured Stalin that the main Allied advance would be south of Berlin.

24. C) Buchenwald and Bergen-Belsen.

25. Holland – food supplies were parachuted into the country to relieve famine.

26. Typhus.

27. Nero Order.

28. B) Torgau, on the river Elbe.

29. The Reichstag.

30. The Reich Chancellery.

31. B) 16 April.

32. The Flight of the Golden Pheasants.

33. The last Allied air raid.

34. Dachau, near Munich.

35. Truth. He was arrested by the SS.

36. Hermann Fegelein.

37. Fiction. The witnesses were Joseph Goebbels and Martin Bormann.

38. Truth. The children were all poisoned.

39. Lüneburg Heath.

40. A) 12 April.

41. Harry Truman.

42. C) Milan.

43. It was to be used as a base for long-range P-51 Mustangs, which were due to take part in a bombing offensive against Japan.

44. Mount Suribachi.

45. C) 4th and 5th Divisions.

46. USS *Bismarck Sea*.

47. Truth. But when the defenders were squeezed back into smaller areas of the island, these *banzai* charges began to occur.

48. A tank that could shoot a jet of flaming liquid.

49. C) 27.

50. Washington D.C. It is the Marine Corps war memorial.

51. C) Less than 300.

52. Okinawa.

53. Battleship Yamato.

54. Truth.

55. The citadel of Shuri.

56. General Simon Bolivar Buckner, Jr.

57. Fiction. Some troops and civilians chose suicide, but for the first time in the Pacific war Japanese soldiers began to surrender peacefully.

58. C) 1,465.

59. B) Cactus Ridge.

60. To lay mines along sea supply routes to the Japanese mainline, ensuring that essential supplies could not reach Japan.

61. Curtis LeMay.

62. The *Fu-Go* were hydrogen balloons, armed with bombs or incendiaries, launched into the Pacific jet stream and intended to reach the US and Canada.

63. B) 50 per cent.

64. Clement Atlee.

65. Demilitarization, De-Nazification, Democratization and Decartelization.

66. Unconditional surrender or prompt and utter destruction.

67. C) Confirmation of a US atomic bomb detonation in the New Mexico desert.

68. The first atomic bomb, nicknamed 'Little Boy'.

69. C) Hiroshima.

70. *Enola Gay*. It was piloted by Colonel Paul W. Tibbets, Jr.

71. Tinian.

72. The Industrial Promotional Hall, Hiroshima.

73. Nagasaki, on 9 August 1945.

74. *Bockscar*, piloted by Major Charles W. Sweeney.

75. Plutonium.

76. The Soviet Union.

77. Truth. The coup failed and the message was broadcast on 15 August, although some forces still continued to fight until September 1945.

78. C) The estimates are 70,000 at Hiroshima and 50,000 at Nagasaki, although more died later from burns and radiation sickness.

79. Douglas MacArthur, on the battleship USS *Missouri*, anchored in Tokyo Bay.

80. A) 55 to 70 million.

81. B) Displaced Person.

82. The Morgenthau Plan.

83. B) That he was not divine.

84. Nuremberg.

85. C) Hermann Göring.

86. Prime Minister Tojo Hideki of Japan.

87. Adolf Eichmann.

88. Odessa.

89. Westminster College in Fulton, Missouri, USA.

90. B) UN General Assembly.

91. War in Vietnam between the Viet Minh and the French, ending in 1954 with division of the country.

92. B) The Marshall Plan.

93. India, which formed into India, Pakistan and Bangladesh.

94. Israel.

95. An air supply to West Berlin following a Soviet blockade of the city.

96. The People's Republic of China.

97. NATO (North Atlantic Treaty Organization) and the Warsaw Pact.

98. The Soviet Union detonated its first atomic bomb.

99. 1949, in May.

100. C) Dachau.

Acknowledgements

I would like to thank all of my colleagues at Imperial War Museums for their support with this book, especially Madeleine James and Julie McMahon. I would also like to thank Louise Dixon and the team at Michael O'Mara Books for the opportunity to take part in this book and for their enthusiasm. Thanks also to my family and friends for their support and encouragement, especially my wife Joanne, who was the ultimate question 'guinea pig'. Finally, I would like to dedicate this book to my mum, a keen quizzer who would have enjoyed the challenge of this one.

Further Reading and Resources

As buyer for the IWM bookshops I have had the privilege of reading many excellent histories on World War II, however the following proved particularly useful during the compilation of this book:

BOOKS

Beevor, Antony, *D-Day: The Battle for Normandy*, Penguin Books, 2010

Beevor, Antony, *Ardennes 1944: Hitler's Last Gamble*, Penguin Books, 2016

Holland, James, *The War in the West – A New History: Germany Ascendant 1939–1941: Volume 1*, Corgi, 2016

Holmes, Richard (Ed.), *World War II: The Definitive Visual Guide*, Dorling Kindersley, 2009

Overy, Richard, *20th Century*, Dorling Kindersley, 2012

Thompson, Julian and Allan Millett, *The Second World War in 100 Objects*, Andre Deutsch, 2012

TV SERIES
The World at War, Thames Television, original TV release 31 October, 1973 to 8 May, 1974

WEB ARTICLES
Imperial War Museums http://www.iwm.org.uk/history

Picture Credits

All images © IWM unless otherwise stated
Maps © David Woodroffe

Chapter 1, Before the War Began
p.8 HU 48179; p.10 MH 13118; p.11 D 2239; p.13 MH 13154;
p.14 HU 39964; p.17 AP 56388; p.19 HU 34656;
p.20 FRA 204717; p.21 HU 7484; p.22 NYP 68062

Chapter 2, Outbreak
p.29 HU 106374; p.31 HU 128051; p.32 GER 18;p.33 HU 55566;
p.34 HU 40003; p.35 A 1; p.36 O 1792; p.41 HU 41241;
p.42 N 375; p.43 MH 29100

Chapter 3, Standing Alone
p.50 CH 19; p.51 CH 1401; p.53 CH 1401; p.54 H 4219; HU 49253;
p.56 HU 76020; p.57 C 5422; p.58 H 5603; p.59 D 2053;
p.61 A 24985; p.63 LN 6194

Chapter 4, Heading South and East
p.71 C 5496; p.72 A 4154; p.73 MH 2620; p.75 MH 24745;
p.78 HU 111384; p.79 FIR 8042, A 4815; p.83 RUS 1206;
p.84 E 4814; p.85 E 10147; p.86 E 3438E

Chapter 5, Widening World War
p.93 MH 6014; p.95 A 6785; p.96 K 758; p.97 NYP 45042;
p.99 NYP 60749; p.100 NY 7343; p.104 E 18980; p.105 E 14640;
p.106 E 18844; p.107 E 14053

Chapter 6, Turning Points
p.114 HU 5152; p.117 FRE 1779; p.118 A 12661;
p.119 A 12671; p.120 NA 142; p.121 STT 9743; p.122 E 21337;
p.125 MAR 583; NA 3437; p.127 CH 16122

Chapter 7, Supreme Leaders
p.133 A 20710; p.134 E 26634; p.135 A 14057; p.136 CH 21121; p.139 HU 51018; p.141 A 24283; p.142 STT 6772N; p.145 NA 5887; p.146 A 17921

Chapter 8, Striking Back
p.153 CNA 2480; p.154 MH 6352; p.155 NA 15141; p.157 NA 11209; p.159 IND 3714; p.161 H 38079; p.162 H 42527; p.164 A 24115; p.165 MH 3660; p.166 B 5593

Chapter 9, Two Fronts
p.173 A 23938; p.174 EA 26319; p.176 CL 449; p.178 MH 1441; p.180 BU 141; p.181 BU 11149; p.183 B 10172; p.185 EA 47958; p.187 EA 49214; p.188 EA 49120

Chapter 10, Endgame and Aftermath
p.195 C 5252; p.196 CH 15714; p.198 BU 2048; p.199 BU 6674; p.200 NYP 57009; p.202 BU 5145; p.203 NYP 57009; p.204 NYF 58685; p.205 NYF 80381; p.207 MH 29427; p.208 MH 2629; p.213 HU 73010